Elements of Literature®

Fifth Course

Holt Adapted Reader

Instruction in Reading Literature and Related Texts

HOLT, RINEHART AND WINSTON

A Harcourt Education Company

Orlando • **Austin** • New York • San Diego • Toronto • London

Contents

Skills Table of Contents

Reading Skills

Literary Skills

Vocabulary Skills

To the Student

A Book for You

Holt Adapted Reader is a book created especially for you. It is a size that's easy to carry around. This book actually tells you to write in it. In addition to outstanding selections and background information you'll find graphic organizers that encourage you to think a different way.

Holt Adapted Reader is designed to accompany *Elements of Literature*. Like *Elements of Literature*, it helps you interact with the literature and background materials.

In *Holt Adapted Reader* you will find two kinds of selections—original literature and adaptations. Original literature is exactly what appears in *Elements of Literature*, Fifth Course. "The Gettysburg Address" and all the poems in this book are examples of original literature. As you read original literature, you will find two kinds of helps— **YOU NEED TO KNOW** and **IN OTHER WORDS**. You Need to Know gives you background information about the work. It also explains some of the work's main ideas. In Other Words summarizes the text that comes before it. That is, it restates the main ideas in different words.

Adaptations are based on stories and other texts that appear in *Elements of Literature*, Fifth Course. Adaptations make the selections more accessible to all readers. You can identify any selection that is an adaptation. Just look for the words *based on* in the Table of Contents.

Reading Literature and Related Materials

When you read a historical essay, you read mainly to get information that is stated directly on the page. When you read literature, you need to go beyond understanding the words on the page. You need to read between the lines of a poem or story to discover the writer's meaning. No matter what kind of reading you do, *Holt Adapted Reader* will help you practice the skills and strategies you need to become an active and successful reader.

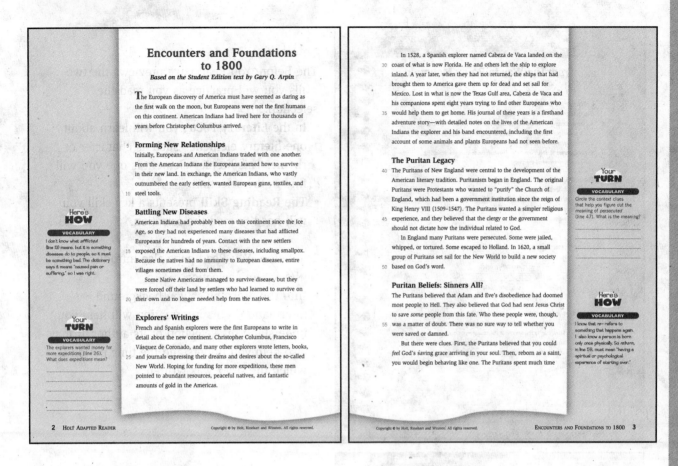

Encounters and Foundations to 1800

Based on the Student Edition text by Gary Q. Arpin

The European discovery of America must have seemed as daring as the first walk on the moon, but Europeans were not the first humans on this continent. American Indians had lived here for thousands of years before Christopher Columbus arrived.

Forming New Relationships

Initially, Europeans and American Indians traded with one another. From the American Indians the Europeans learned how to survive in their new land. In exchange, the American Indians, who vastly outnumbered the early settlers, wanted European guns, textiles, and steel tools.

Battling New Diseases

American Indians had probably been on this continent since the Ice Age, so they had not experienced many diseases that had afflicted Europeans for hundreds of years. Contact with the new settlers exposed the American Indians to these diseases, including smallpox. Because the natives had no immunity to European diseases, entire villages sometimes died from them.

Some Native Americans managed to survive disease, but they were forced off their land by settlers who had learned to survive on their own and no longer needed help from the natives.

Explorers' Writings

French and Spanish explorers were the first Europeans to write in detail about the new continent. Christopher Columbus, Francisco Vásquez de Coronado, and many other explorers wrote letters, books, and journals expressing their dreams and desires about the so-called New World. Hoping for funding for more expeditions, these men pointed to abundant resources, peaceful natives, and fantastic amounts of gold in the Americas.

In 1528, a Spanish explorer named Cabeza de Vaca landed on the coast of what is now Florida. He and others left the ship to explore inland. A year later, when they had not returned, the ships that had brought them to America gave them up for dead and set sail for Mexico. Lost in what is now the Texas Gulf area, Cabeza de Vaca and his companions spent eight years trying to find other Europeans who would help them to get home. His journal of these years is a firsthand adventure story—with detailed notes on the lives of the American Indians the explorer and his band encountered, including the first account of some animals and plants Europeans had not seen before.

The Puritan Legacy

The Puritans of New England were central to the development of the American literary tradition. Puritanism began in England. The original Puritans were Protestants who wanted to "purify" the Church of England, which had been a government institution since the reign of King Henry VIII (1509–1547). The Puritans wanted a simpler religious experience, and they believed that the clergy or the government should not dictate how the individual related to God.

In England many Puritans were persecuted. Some were jailed, whipped, or tortured. Some escaped to Holland. In 1620, a small group of Puritans set sail for the New World to build a new society based on God's word.

Puritan Beliefs: Sinners All?

The Puritans believed that Adam and Eve's disobedience had doomed most people to Hell. They also believed that God had sent Jesus Christ to save *some* people from this fate. Who these people were, though, was a matter of doubt. There was no sure way to tell whether you were saved or damned.

But there were clues. First, the Puritans believed that you could *feel* God's saving grace arriving in your soul. Then, reborn as a saint, you would begin behaving like one. The Puritans spent much time

Here's HOW
VOCABULARY
I don't know what *afflicted* (line 13) means, but it is something diseases do to people, so it must be something bad. The dictionary says it means "caused pain or suffering," so I was right.

Your TURN
VOCABULARY
The explorers wanted money for more *expeditions* (line 26). What does *expeditions* mean?

Your TURN
VOCABULARY
Circle the context clues that help you figure out the meaning of *persecuted* (line 47). What is the meaning?

Here's HOW
VOCABULARY
I know that *re-* refers to something that happens again. I also know a person is born only once physically. So *reborn*, in line 59, must mean "having a spiritual or psychological experience of starting over."

Historical Introductions

An introduction is provided for each literary period covered: Encounters and Foundations to 1800; American Romanticism: 1800–1860; American Masters: Whitman and Dickinson; The Rise of Realism: The Civil War to 1914; The Moderns: 1914–1939; and Contemporary Literature: 1939 to Present. Side notes and footnotes focus on building vocabulary.

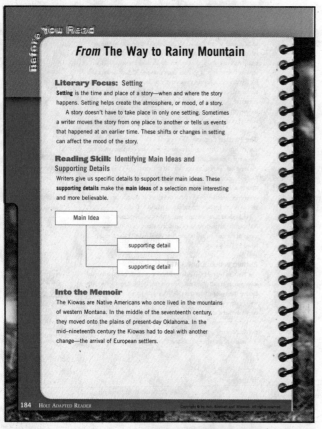

Before You Read

The Before You Read page previews the two skills you will practice as you read the selection.

- In the **Literary Focus** you will learn about one literary element—such as character or rhyme. This literary element is one you will find in the selection.
- The **Reading Skill** presents a key skill you will need to read the selection.

The Before You Read page also introduces you to the reading selection.

- **Into the Story** gives you background information. This information will help you understand the selection or its author. It may also help you understand the time period in which the story was written.

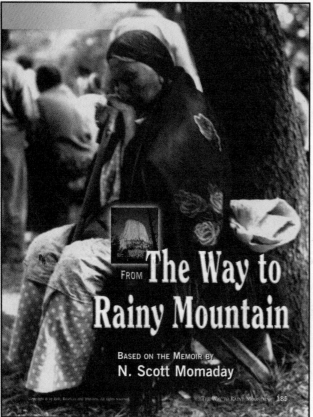

Interactive Selections from *Elements of Literature*

The literary selections are either original selections or adaptations of selections from *Elements of Literature,* Fifth Course. The selections are printed to give you room to mark up the text.

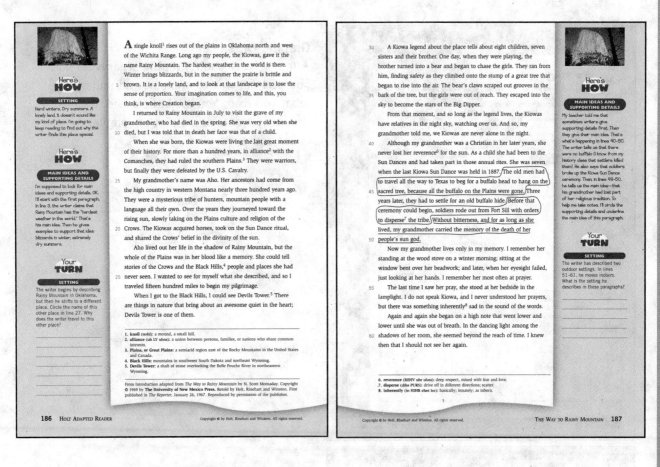

Here's HOW

SETTING

Hard winters. Dry summers. A lonely land. It doesn't sound like my kind of place. I'm going to keep reading to find out why the writer finds this place special.

Here's HOW

MAIN IDEAS AND SUPPORTING DETAILS

I'm supposed to look for main ideas and supporting details. OK, I'll start with the first paragraph. In line 3, the writer claims that Rainy Mountain has the "hardest weather in the world." That's his main idea. Then he gives examples to support that idea: blizzards in winter, extremely dry summers.

Your TURN

SETTING

The writer begins by describing Rainy Mountain in Oklahoma, but then he shifts to a different place. Circle the name of this other place in line 27. Why does the writer travel to this other place?

_____

_____

_____

A single knoll[1] rises out of the plains in Oklahoma north and west of the Wichita Range. Long ago my people, the Kiowas, gave it the name Rainy Mountain. The hardest weather in the world is there. Winter brings blizzards, but in the summer the prairie is brittle and brown. It is a lonely land, and to look at that landscape is to lose the sense of proportion. Your imagination comes to life, and this, you think, is where Creation began.

I returned to Rainy Mountain in July to visit the grave of my grandmother, who had died in the spring. She was very old when she died, but I was told that in death her face was that of a child.

When she was born, the Kiowas were living the last great moment of their history. For more than a hundred years, in alliance[2] with the Comanches, they had ruled the southern Plains.[3] They were warriors, but finally they were defeated by the U.S. Cavalry.

My grandmother's name was Aho. Her ancestors had come from the high country in western Montana nearly three hundred years ago. They were a mysterious tribe of hunters, mountain people with a language all their own. Over the years they journeyed toward the rising sun, slowly taking on the Plains culture and religion of the Crows. The Kiowas acquired horses, took on the Sun Dance ritual, and shared the Crows' belief in the divinity of the sun.

Aho lived out her life in the shadow of Rainy Mountain, but the whole of the Plains was in her blood like a memory. She could tell stories of the Crows and the Black Hills,[4] people and places she had never seen. I wanted to see for myself what she described, and so I traveled fifteen hundred miles to begin my pilgrimage.

When I got to the Black Hills, I could see Devils Tower.[5] There are things in nature that bring about an awesome quiet in the heart; Devils Tower is one of them.

1. **knoll** (nohl): a mound, a small hill.
2. **alliance** (uh LY uhns): a union between persons, families, or nations who share common interests.
3. **Plains, or Great Plains:** a semiarid region east of the Rocky Mountains in the United States and Canada.
4. **Black Hills:** mountains in southwest South Dakota and northeast Wyoming.
5. **Devils Tower:** a shaft of stone overlooking the Belle Fouche River in northeastern Wyoming.

From Introduction adapted from *The Way to Rainy Mountain* by N. Scott Momaday. Copyright © 1969 by **The University of New Mexico Press.** Retold by Holt, Rinehart and Winston. First published in *The Reporter,* January 26, 1967. Reproduced by permission of the publisher.

A Kiowa legend about the place tells about eight children, seven sisters and their brother. One day, when they were playing, the brother turned into a bear and began to chase the girls. They ran from him, finding safety as they climbed onto the stump of a great tree that began to rise into the air. The bear's claws scraped out grooves in the bark of the tree, but the girls were out of reach. They escaped into the sky to become the stars of the Big Dipper.

From that moment, and so long as the legend lives, the Kiowas have relatives in the night sky, watching over us. And so, my grandmother told me, we Kiowas are never alone in the night.

Although my grandmother was a Christian in her later years, she never lost her reverence[6] for the sun. As a child she had been to the Sun Dances and had taken part in those annual rites. She was seven when the last Kiowa Sun Dance was held in 1887. The old men had to travel all the way to Texas to beg for a buffalo head to hang on the sacred tree, because all the buffalo on the Plains were gone. Three years later, they had to settle for an old buffalo hide. Before that ceremony could begin, soldiers rode out from Fort Sill with orders to disperse[7] the tribe. Without bitterness, and for as long as she lived, my grandmother carried the memory of the death of her people's sun god.

Now my grandmother lives only in my memory. I remember her standing at the wood stove on a winter morning; sitting at the window bent over her beadwork; and later, when her eyesight failed, just looking at her hands. I remember her most often at prayer.

The last time I saw her pray, she stood at her bedside in the lamplight. I did not speak Kiowa, and I never understood her prayers, but there was something inherently[8] sad in the sound of the words.

Again and again she began on a high note that went lower and lower until she was out of breath. In the dancing light among the shadows of her room, she seemed beyond the reach of time. I knew then that I should not see her again.

6. **reverence** (REHV uhr uhns): deep respect, mixed with fear and love.
7. **disperse** (dihs PURS): drive off in different directions; scatter.
8. **inherently** (in HIHR ehnt lee): basically; innately; as inborn.

Here's HOW

MAIN IDEAS AND SUPPORTING DETAILS

My teacher told me that sometimes writers give supporting details first. Then they give their main idea. That's what's happening in lines 40–50. The writer tells us that there were no buffalo (I know from my history class that settlers killed them). He also says that soldiers broke up the Kiowa Sun Dance ceremony. Then, in lines 48–50, he tells us the main idea—that his grandmother had lost part of her religious tradition. To help me take notes, I'll circle the supporting details and underline the main idea of this paragraph.

Your TURN

SETTING

The writer has described two outdoor settings. In lines 51–61, he moves indoors. What is the setting he describes in these paragraphs?

_____

_____

_____

Strategies to Guide Your Reading: Side Notes

The **Here's HOW** feature models, or shows you, how to apply a particular skill to what you are reading. This feature lets you see how another person might think about the text. Each Here's HOW focuses on a reading skill, a literary skill, or a vocabulary skill.

The **Your TURN** feature gives you a chance to practice a skill on your own. Each Your TURN focuses on a reading skill, a literary skill, or a vocabulary skill. You might be asked to underline or circle words in the text. You might also be asked to write your response to a question on lines that are provided for you.

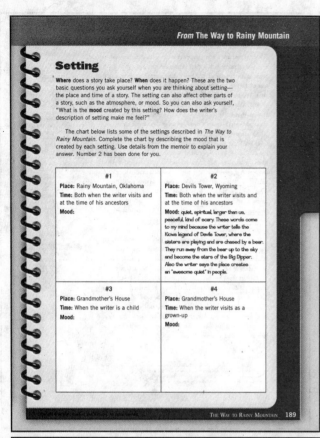

Graphic Organizers

After each selection, **graphic organizers** give you a visual way to organize and understand what you read. You might be asked to chart the main events of the plot or complete a cause-and-effect chain.

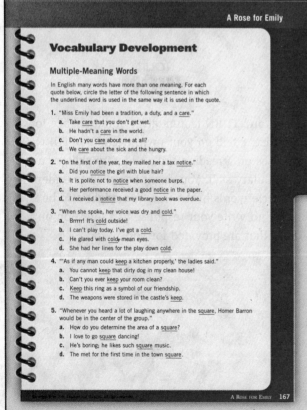

Vocabulary Development

Vocabulary Development worksheets appear at the end of some literary selections. These worksheets check your knowledge of words used in the selection and help you develop skills for vocabulary building.

Holt Adapted Reader

Instruction in Reading Literature and Related Texts

Encounters and Foundations to 1800

Based on the Student Edition text by Gary Q. Arpin

The European discovery of America must have seemed as daring as the first walk on the moon, but Europeans were not the first humans on this continent. American Indians had lived here for thousands of years before Christopher Columbus arrived.

Forming New Relationships

Initially, Europeans and American Indians traded with one another. From the American Indians the Europeans learned how to survive in their new land. In exchange, the American Indians, who vastly outnumbered the early settlers, wanted European guns, textiles, and 10 steel tools.

Battling New Diseases

American Indians had probably been on this continent since the Ice Age, so they had not experienced many diseases that had afflicted Europeans for hundreds of years. Contact with the new settlers 15 exposed the American Indians to these diseases, including smallpox. Because the natives had no immunity to European diseases, entire villages sometimes died from them.

Some Native Americans managed to survive disease, but they were forced off their land by settlers who had learned to survive on 20 their own and no longer needed help from the natives.

Explorers' Writings

French and Spanish explorers were the first Europeans to write in detail about the new continent. Christopher Columbus, Francisco Vásquez de Coronado, and many other explorers wrote letters, books, 25 and journals expressing their dreams and desires about the so-called New World. Hoping for funding for more expeditions, these men pointed to abundant resources, peaceful natives, and fantastic amounts of gold in the Americas.

Here's HOW

VOCABULARY

I don't know what *afflicted* (line 13) means, but it is something diseases do to people, so it must be something bad. The dictionary says it means "caused pain or suffering," so I was right.

Your TURN

VOCABULARY

The explorers wanted money for more expeditions (line 26). What does *expeditions* mean?

_____

_____

_____

_____

In 1528, a Spanish explorer named Cabeza de Vaca landed on the
30 coast of what is now Florida. He and others left the ship to explore
inland. A year later, when they had not returned, the ships that had
brought them to America gave them up for dead and set sail for
Mexico. Lost in what is now the Texas Gulf area, Cabeza de Vaca and
his companions spent eight years trying to find other Europeans who
35 would help them to get home. His journal of these years is a firsthand
adventure story—with detailed notes on the lives of the American
Indians the explorer and his band encountered, including the first
account of some animals and plants Europeans had not seen before.

The Puritan Legacy

40 The Puritans of New England were central to the development of the
American literary tradition. Puritanism began in England. The original
Puritans were Protestants who wanted to "purify" the Church of
England, which had been a government institution since the reign of
King Henry VIII (1509–1547). The Puritans wanted a simpler religious
45 experience, and they believed that the clergy or the government
should not dictate how the individual related to God.

In England many Puritans were persecuted. Some were jailed,
whipped, or tortured. Some escaped to Holland. In 1620, a small
group of Puritans set sail for the New World to build a new society
50 based on God's word.

Puritan Beliefs: Sinners All?

The Puritans believed that Adam and Eve's disobedience had doomed
most people to Hell. They also believed that God had sent Jesus Christ
to save *some* people from this fate. Who these people were, though,
55 was a matter of doubt. There was no sure way to tell whether you
were saved or damned.

But there were clues. First, the Puritans believed that you could
feel God's saving grace arriving in your soul. Then, reborn as a saint,
you would begin behaving like one. The Puritans spent much time

VOCABULARY

Circle the context clues
that help you figure out the
meaning of *persecuted*
(line 47). What is the meaning?

_____

_____

_____

_____

VOCABULARY

I know that *re–* refers to
something that happens again.
I also know a person is born
only once physically. So *reborn*,
in line 58, must mean "having a
spiritual or psychological
experience of starting over."

60 examining their lives for signs of grace. They also relied on themselves and worked hard—the very qualities needed for building a new society.

Puritan Politics: Government by Contract

The Puritans believed that God and humankind were bound together
65 by a covenant, or contract. They also believed that people should make similar agreements among themselves. Onboard the ship *Mayflower* the Puritans wrote and signed the Mayflower Compact. It stated how the group would be governed once they landed. This idea of a government by contract was later adopted in the American
70 Constitution.

But the Puritans were not democratic. They believed that individuals who were saved should govern those who were not saved and protect the community from evil. In 1692, the people of Salem, Massachusetts, grew convinced that witches lived among them. Afraid
75 that the morals of the town were weakening, they accused one hundred fifty of their fellow townspeople of witchcraft, and nineteen of those were hanged.

The Bible in America

The Puritans read the Bible as the story of the creation, fall, and
80 rescue of the human race. Each Puritan could see connections between biblical events and his or her own life. The Bible was a guidebook for each person's spiritual journey.

To the Puritans the Bible was also the literal word of God. It was important to be able to read the Bible and to follow religious debates.
85 Therefore, the Puritans valued education. Harvard College was founded, in 1636, as a school for ministers. Three years later, the first printing press in the American Colonies was set up.

Puritans' beliefs required that they keep a close watch on their spiritual lives. This focus reveals itself in their diaries and histories,
90 which were written to record the workings of God.

Characteristics of Puritan Writing

- The Bible was a model for Puritan writing. Puritans saw connections between biblical events and their own lives.
- Diaries and histories were the most common forms of Puritan
95   writing.
- Puritans favored a plain, clear writing style.

The Age of Reason: Tinkerers and Experimenters

The Age of Reason began in Europe in the 1600s and 1700s. Certain thinkers known as **rationalists** believed that human beings could use
100 their reason to find truth.

The Puritans saw God as active in human affairs. The rationalists saw God differently. The great English rationalist Sir Isaac Newton (1642–1727) compared God to a clockmaker. Having created the universe, God then left it to run on its own. God's special gift to
105 people was reason. Reason enabled each person to direct his or her own life.

While rationalist theory took shape in Europe, scientific experimenting thrived in the American Colonies. From the earliest days, Americans had to be tinkerers; they had to make do with what
110 they had, and they had to achieve results.

The Smallpox Plague

In April 1721, a ship from the West Indies docked in Boston Harbor. It carried sugar and molasses. It also carried smallpox.

At that time, smallpox was one of the miseries of life, much as
115 AIDS is today. The disease spread rapidly and often killed its victims.

When smallpox began to spread through Boston in June 1721, a man named Cotton Mather (1663–1728) spoke up. This Puritan minister was also a scientist, and he had heard of a method for dealing with smallpox. The method, called **inoculation,** had been
120 developed by a physician in Turkey.

VOCABULARY

Use context clues to figure out the meaning of *tinkerers* (line 109). Write the definition on the lines below.

_____

_____

_____

_____

VOCABULARY

I just checked a dictionary and learned that an *inoculation* (line 119) is a type of shot. It gives a person a mild case of a disease and so prevents a more serious case.

Boston's doctors strongly opposed the idea of inoculation, especially because it came from a Muslim. A debate raged for most of the year. Tempers flared. Mather's house was even bombed.

Nevertheless, Mather inoculated nearly three hundred people.
125 By March 1722, only six of these had died. Inoculation worked.

The smallpox conflict shows that Americans could be contradictory. Mather, for example, was a devout Puritan but also a practical scientist. His approach to the smallpox epidemic also shows that it was necessary to be practical in America. Frontier farmers
130 shared something with scientists like Mather: They had to use the few tools they had available to achieve results. A willingness to experiment was necessary to the public welfare.

Deism: Are People Basically Good?

Like the Puritans, the rationalists saw God in the natural world.
135 Unlike the Puritans, though, they believed that *all* people at *all* times could discover God's natural laws.

This outlook, called **deism,** was shared by many thinkers, including many founders of the American nation. Unlike the Puritans, deists viewed people as basically good. They believed that people
140 could use reason to perfect themselves and society. The best way to perfect society and to worship God was to do good for others. Deism made concern for the common good one of the nation's highest goals.

These rationalist ideas helped fuel the American struggle for independence. They also helped to shape the Declaration of
145 Independence.

The Rationalist Worldview

- People find truth through reason.
- God created the universe but is not active in it.
- The natural world follows God's laws, which can be discovered
150 through reason.
- People are basically good.
- The best form of worship is helping others.
- Humans show progress toward greater perfection.

VOCABULARY

If Mather, who was both religious and practical, is an example of a contradictory (line 127) American, *contradictory* must have to do with opposites. The dictionary shows I was close. It gives the meaning "inconsistent."

VOCABULARY

Consider what you know about the word *fuel* as a source of energy for heat or power. Then, explain the use of "fuel" in the sentence in lines 143–144.

_____

_____

_____

6 HOLT ADAPTED READER

Self-made Americans

155 In the American Colonies the written word served mainly practical
or political purposes. This remained true after the Revolutionary War
(1775–1783). A new nation was being established, and there was
work to be done.

The Autobiography of Benjamin Franklin is a masterpiece of the
160 American Age of Reason. For his autobiography, Franklin (1706–1790)
used a popular Puritan form—writing about oneself. However,
Franklin's work was not religious. His story of a self-made American
would become the model for some classic American literature and for
many bestsellers today.

Here Follow Some Verses upon the Burning of Our House, July 10, 1666

Literary Focus: The Plain Style

In their style of writing, as well as in their manner of worship, the Puritans favored the plain and unornamented. Though the plain style now seems hard to read, in the 1600s, it was considered simple and direct. The **plain style** emphasized simple sentences and the use of everyday words from common speech.

Although Anne Bradstreet uses figures of speech in her poetry, her writing is still influenced by strong, simple Puritan style. In the poem, Bradstreet records her journey from grief to spiritual comfort.

Reading Skill: Analyzing Text Structures: Inversion

This poem is filled with inversions. In an inversion the words of a sentence or phrase are taken out of our normal English syntax, or word order: "In silent night when rest I took," instead of "In silent night when I took rest." In earlier English poetry, poets frequently used inversion to maintain the pattern of a rhyme.

Into the Poem

Anne Bradstreet's poetry was greatly influenced by her Puritan religious beliefs. In 1630, Anne, her husband, Simon, and Anne's father journeyed across the Atlantic to live in New England. There, Anne raised a family of eight children and still found time to write poetry. Anne never attempted to publish her poetry herself, as that would have seemed too proud. When Anne's first book was published without her permission, the praise it received encouraged her to continue writing for the rest of her life.

ANNE BRADSTREET

Here Follow Some Verses upon the Burning of Our House, July 10, 1666

Anne Bradstreet

Here's HOW

INVERSION

In lines 1–2, I see how the inversions make the words at the end of the lines rhyme (took; look). In normal word order the lines read: "In silent night when I took rest / I did not look for sorrow near."

Your TURN

INVERSION

Re-read line 7. Now, circle the inverted words. Then, draw an arrow showing where those words would be located in normal English word order. Rewrite the new word order below.

_____

_____

_____

_____

Here's HOW

PLAIN STYLE

When I read lines 13–15, I can tell this poem is in plain style. The speaker states ideas in clear and simple language.

YOU NEED TO KNOW Awakened by shouts of "Fire!" the speaker escapes from her burning house and then watches flames consume it. When she later passes the ruins, she scolds herself for mourning the loss of her worldly goods. She reminds herself that God gave her those goods and has justly taken them away. She concludes by stating that her true house, hope, and treasure lie in heaven.

In silent night when rest I took
For sorrow near I did not look
I wakened was with thund'ring noise
And piteous[1] shrieks of dreadful voice.
5 That fearful sound of "Fire!" and "Fire!"
Let no man know is my desire.
I, starting up, the light did spy,
And to my God my heart did cry
To strengthen me in my distress
10 And not to leave me succorless.[2]

IN OTHER WORDS It was a quiet night. I slept peacefully, never expecting anything bad to happen. Then, suddenly I woke to the sound of loud noises and screams of "Fire!" It was a sound I hope on one has to hear. I sat up and saw the light of the fire. My heart cried out to God, asking him to give me strength and not to leave me without help or comfort.

Then, coming out, beheld a space
The flame consume[3] my dwelling place.
And when I could no longer look,
I blest His name that gave and took,[4]
15 That laid my goods[5] now in the dust.
Yea, so it was, and so 'twas just.

---

1. **piteous** (PIHT ee uhs): deserving sympathy; to be pitied.
2. **succorless** (SUHK uhr lihs): without aid or assistance; helpless.
3. **consume** (kuhn SOOM): burn up.
4. **that gave and took:** reference to the Bible verse Job 1:21: "The Lord gave, and the Lord hath taken away; blessed be the name of the Lord."
5. **goods:** belongings.

It was His own, it was not mine,

Far be it that I should repine;[6]

He might of all justly bereft

20　But yet sufficient for us left.

IN OTHER WORDS Outside, I watched my house burn down. When I couldn't stand the sight any longer, I blessed God, who both gives and takes away, and who left all I owned in ashes. It was fair because it all belonged to God, not me. I shouldn't whine: After all, God had the right to take everything away, but he left us enough.

When by the ruins oft I past

My sorrowing eyes aside did cast,

And here and there the places spy[7]

Where oft I sat and long did lie:

25　Here stood that trunk, and there that chest,

There lay that store[8] I counted best.

My pleasant things in ashes lie,

And them behold no more shall I.

Under thy roof no guest shall sit,

30　Nor at thy table eat a bit.

No pleasant tale shall e'er be told,

Nor things recounted[9] done of old.

No candle e'er shall shine in thee,

Nor bridegroom's voice e'er heard shall be.

35　In silence ever shall thou lie,

Adieu,[10] Adieu, all's vanity.[11]

Here's HOW

VOCABULARY

If I read lines 19–20 closely, I think I can figure out the meaning of the word *bereft* (line 19). Both lines have inversions, so I will change the lines to normal word order: "He might [have] justly bereft [us] of all / But yet [He] left sufficient for us." I know *sufficient* means "enough," and the word *but* tells me that *bereft* will be the opposite of "left us enough." So I think *bereft of all* means "taken away everything." I checked a dictionary, and I guessed the meaning correctly.

Your TURN

PLAIN STYLE

Read lines 27–30. Do you think these lines have been written in plain style? Why or why not? Give an example to support your opinion.

_____

_____

_____

_____

_____

_____

_____

_____

---

　6. **repine** (rih PYN): complain.

　7. **spy:** see.

　8. **store:** things put away for the future.

　9. **recounted** (rih KOWNT ihd): told about.

10. **Adieu** (uh DYOO): French for "goodbye."

11. **all's vanity:** reference to the Bible verse Ecclesiastes 12:8: "Vanity of vanities, saith the preacher; all is vanity." This verse ends a famous description of the approach of death (Ecclesiastes 12:1–7).

Reproduced by kind permission of the vicar and church wardens of St. Botolph's Church, Boston, England.

Read line 52, noting the word *pelf*, and then read its footnote at the bottom of the page. Why do you suppose Bradstreet uses such a bitter word to describe her possessions?

_____

_____

_____

_____

_____

The last two lines of the poem contain a tricky inversion. Bradstreet places "The world" before "no longer let me love." This could mean that the world no longer allowed her to love. But here it means something else. She rhymes *love* with *above*, emphasizing that she is not to love the world, but rather God and his heaven.

IN OTHER WORDS   I often walked by my ruined house and looked at the familiar spots—where I sat, where a trunk or a chest stood, where my favorite possessions lay. All these fine things are burned to ashes, and I will never see them again. My house! No guest will sit under your roof or eat at your table again. No one will tell stories in you or talk about old times. No candle will shine in your windows, and no bridegroom's voice will be heard. You will lie in silence forever. Goodbye, house—possessions have no real worth.

Then straight I 'gin my heart to chide,[12]
And did thy wealth on earth abide?[13]
Didst fix thy hope on mold'ring[14] dust?
40 The arm of flesh didst make thy trust?
Raise up thy thoughts above the sky
That dunghill[15] mists away may fly.
Thou hast an house on high erect,
Framed[16] by that mighty Architect,
45 With glory richly furnished,
Stands permanent though this be fled.
It's purchased and paid for too
By Him who hath enough to do.
A price so vast as is unknown
50 Yet by His gift is made thine own;
There's wealth enough, I need no more,
Farewell, my pelf,[17] farewell my store.
The world no longer let me love,
My hope and treasure lies above.

---

12. **chide** (chyd): to scold; find fault with.
13. **abide** (uh BYD): wait; stay.
14. **mold'ring:** short for moldering (MOHL duhr ihng): breaking up and wasting away.
15. **dunghill:** pile of dung or manure.
16. **framed:** put together; constructed; formed.
17. **pelf** (pehlf): wealth or worldly goods; sometimes used as a term of contempt because the goods are considered to be ill-gotten or even stolen.

IN OTHER WORDS   Then right away I began to scold my heart: Was your treasure here on earth? Did you fix your hopes on things that turn to dust? Did you trust in the human body, which is mortal? Raise your thoughts higher so the mists that cloud your thinking will fly away. You have a house that stands high above, built by a great architect and filled with glory. That house lasts forever, though the one on earth is gone. That house was bought by Jesus with his life, a price higher than anyone can know, and yet he gives it to you as a gift. That's all the wealth I need; goodbye to my earthly belongings. I will no longer love things of this world; my hope and treasure are in heaven.

Poetic Inversion

Poets in Anne Bradstreet's time often used a grammatical device called **inversion.** This device allows the word order to be reversed (or inverted) in order for the lines to rhyme.

In the left-hand side of the chart below are examples of poetic inversion. Read these examples carefully. Then, "translate" each phrase into its ordinary, natural word order. One inversion has been done for you.

Inversion from the Poem	Normal Word Order
1. "when rest I took" (line 1)	
2. "I wakened was" (line 3)	
3. "My pleasant things in ashes lie" (line 27)	My pleasant things lie in ashes
4. "And them behold no more shall I" (line 28)	

Vocabulary Development

Context Clues

When you do not understand a word in a sentence, you may find a clue in the surrounding words, or context. These context clues can help you understand the meaning of the word that you don't know. Use context clues in each of the following sentences to decide which word in parentheses correctly completes the sentence. Circle the correct word, and underline any context clues that helped you arrive at your answer. One has been done for you.

1. The <u>poor, hungry</u> kitten was mewing (*happily,* (*piteously*)) at the back door, so I let it in.

2. We stood and watched as the blazing fire spread to the roof of the house and then (*consumed, recounted*) the whole building.

3. In the children's game of hide-and-seek, when the boy saw anyone hiding, he called out, "I (*spy, abide*) you hiding there!"

4. There were boxes and bags of food in the cabin, a great (*store, pelf*) of provisions that would see us through the winter.

5. We are building a new house; the builder (*chided, framed*) its walls in only one week.

From Sinners in the Hands of an Angry God

Literary Focus: Figures of Speech

Figures of speech describe one thing in terms of another, very different thing. Sometimes the word *like* or *as* signals a figure of speech. Jonathan Edwards uses figures of speech to compare God's anger to ordinary, everyday things that his listeners could relate to and understand.

Reading Skill: Finding the Main Idea

The **main idea** is the most important idea in a piece of writing. Main ideas are sometimes, but not always, stated directly. When a writer doesn't state the main idea, it's up to you to figure it out. You have to use details in the text to infer, or guess, what larger idea the writer is getting at. Listing key words and details as you read can help you find the main idea.

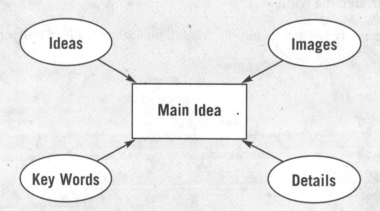

Into the Sermon

This is Edwards's most famous sermon, which he delivered on a visit to a church in Enfield, Connecticut, in 1741. The "natural men" he was trying to reach with his sermon were those in the congregation who had not been "born again." That is, they had not accepted Jesus as their savior. Edwards's sermon had a powerful effect; several times he had to ask his shrieking and fainting audience for quiet.

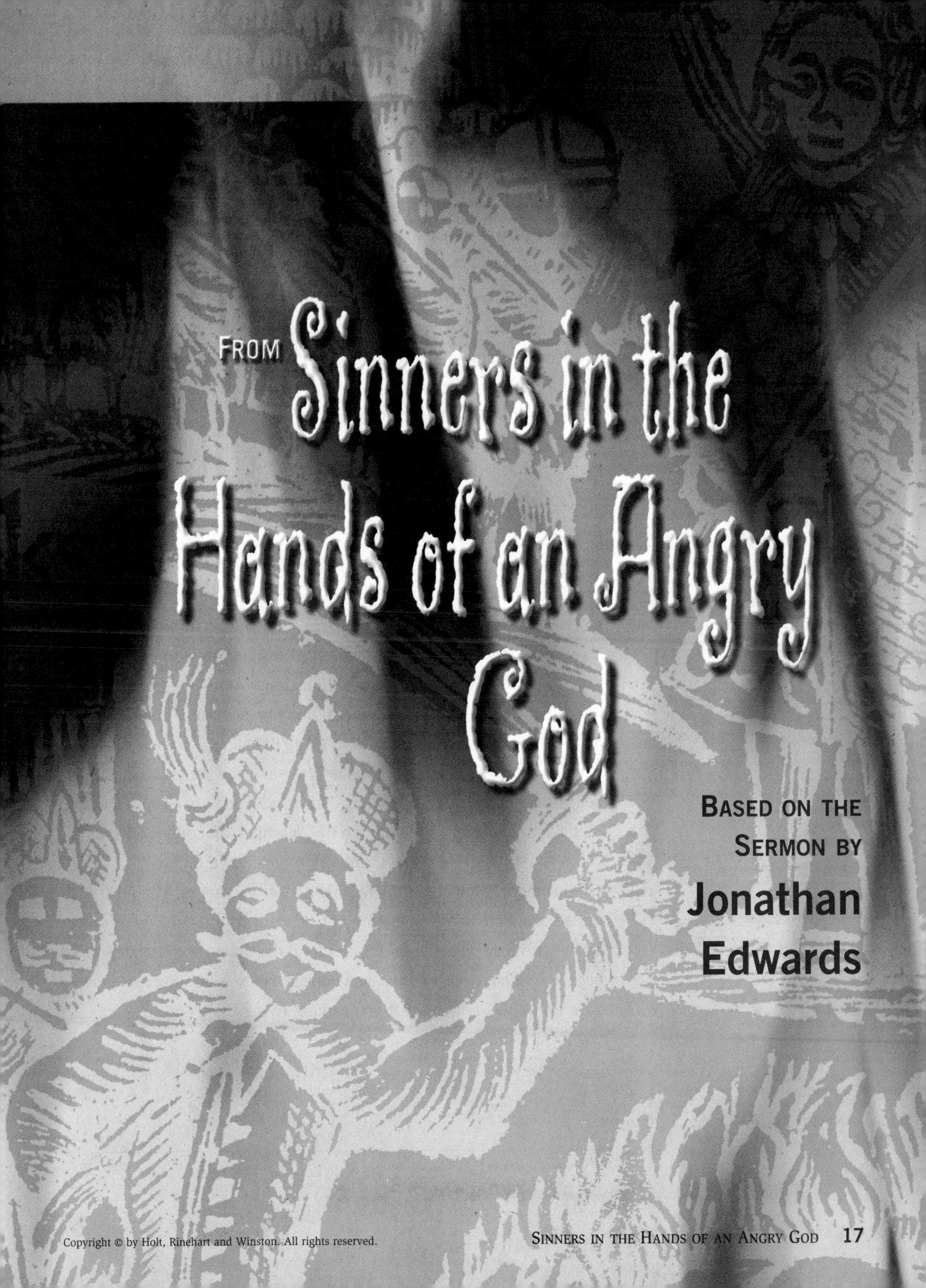

FROM **Sinners in the Hands of an Angry God**

BASED ON THE
SERMON BY
**Jonathan
Edwards**

Here's

FIGURE OF SPEECH

In lines 13–16, I think Edwards's comparison of God's wrath to water behind a dam is a figure of speech. It makes me realize how powerful Edwards thinks God's anger is.

Here's

FINDING THE MAIN IDEA

The main idea in lines 20–27 seems to be that it is only God's mercy that keeps me from being dropped into hell.

Your

FIGURE OF SPEECH

What are the figures of speech in lines 28–29? Underline the phrases.

Your

FINDING THE MAIN IDEA

What do you think is the main idea of Edwards's sermon? Write your answer on the lines below.

_____

_____

_____

_____

Natural men are held in the hand of God, suspended over the pit of hell. The devil is waiting for them, hell is opening up for them, and the flames gather and flash about them and will swallow them up. The only thing that can save them is a God who is angry with them.

5   I will use this awful subject to wake up people in this congregation who have not accepted Christ as their savior.

    You know you are kept out of hell, but you do not know that it is only God that keeps you safe. You think instead that it is your good health and your concern for your own life.

10   Your wickedness makes you as heavy as lead. If God lets you go, you will sink into the bottomless gulf. Nothing will hold you up, just as a spider's web will not stop a falling rock.

    God's wrath° is like waters that are dammed up. As long as you do evil, the waters rise and grow mighty. God saves you by holding

15 the waters back. But if God removes his hand, the fiery floods of his fury will rush out and destroy you.

    The bow of God's wrath is bent, and justice bends the arrow at your heart and strains the bow. It is only the mere pleasure of God that keeps the arrow from being made drunk with your blood.

20   God, who holds you over the fiery pit just as you would hold a disgusting insect over a fire, is dreadfully angry. You are ten thousand times more horrible in His eyes than the most poisonous snake. It was only God's hand that kept you from going to hell as you slept last night. It is only God's hand that has kept you from being dropped into

25 hell since you got up this morning. Only God's hand has kept you out of the fiery pit as you sit in church this morning, and only God's hand keeps you at this very moment from dropping down into hell.

    O sinner! Think about the terrible danger you are in. The great furnace of wrath is full of the fire of God's anger. You hang over it by

30 a slender thread. The flames flash around the thread and threaten to burn it. You have no way to save yourself. There is nothing that you have ever done, nothing that you can do, to persuade God to spare you for one moment.

° **wrath:** anger; rage.

Figures of Speech

Figures of speech describe one thing in terms of another, very different thing. Writers often use figures of speech when discussing abstract ideas. For example, describing *liberty* as an unlocked cage can help the reader understand the abstract idea more clearly. To help his listeners understand his sermon, Edwards uses figures of speech to compare God's wrath to ordinary, everyday things.

Explore Edwards's figures of speech by completing the chart below. The first one has been done for you.

Edwards's Figure of Speech	Meaning
1. "Your wickedness makes you as heavy as lead. If God lets you go, you will sink into the bottomless gulf." (lines 10–11)	You are like lead because sin has made you so heavy. If lead is thrown into water, it sinks. Therefore, if God lets go of you, you will sink into hell.
2. "God's wrath is like waters that are dammed up. . . . God saves you by holding the waters back. But if God removes His hand, the fiery floods of his fury will rush out and destroy you." (lines 13–16)	
3. "The bow of God's wrath is bent, and justice bends the arrow at your heart and strains the bow." (lines 17–18)	
4. "God, who holds you over the fiery pit just as you would hold a disgusting insect over a fire, is dreadfully angry." (lines 20–21)	

From The Autobiography

Literary Focus: First-Person Point of View

An autobiography tells the story of the writer's life. Benjamin Franklin writes his story using the pronoun *I*, from the **first-person point of view.** A first-person point of view shows events from the narrator's perspective. When a story is told from the first-person point of view, two important things happen. First, we share directly in the narrator's thoughts and feelings. Second, we know only what the narrator knows.

Reading Skill: Making Inferences

Making inferences is a lot like being a detective. You use your own experiences and knowledge as well as evidence from the text to make inferences, or educated guesses, about what is happening.

Evidence
Franklin gave what little money he had to some people on the boat.

Knowledge
Giving money away is generous.

My Experience
My brother gave me the money I needed to buy a new CD.

Inference
Franklin is a generous man. He is willing to help people who need money.

Into the Autobiography

Franklin began *The Autobiography* when he was sixty-five. He continued working on it off and on until his death, at eighty-four, leaving it unfinished. The following excerpt begins when Franklin was a teenager and living in Boston. He was working as an apprentice to his older brother James, who printed a newspaper. The brothers argued, and the younger Franklin decided to flee Boston for Philadelphia. He was escaping a contract of service that his brother had forced him to sign.

Benjamin Franklin

BASED ON The Autobiography

FIRST-PERSON POINT OF VIEW

As I read line 2, I notice Benjamin Franklin's use of the pronoun *I*. That means I will see events through Franklin's eyes. Anything he says will be from his point of view alone.

MAKING INFERENCES

In lines 2–5, Franklin describes himself as dirty and hungry. He says that this is unlike the person he is now. I can infer that Franklin is now clean, well-dressed, and well-fed.

FIRST-PERSON POINT OF VIEW

In lines 14–17, circle any information that only the narrator could have known.

MAKING INFERENCES

What can you infer from the subhead "Arriving at Moral Perfection" in line 18? What does it tell you about Franklin?

_____

_____

_____

_____

Arrival in Philadelphia

I am telling you about the many hardships I experienced during this time so that you can compare my unlikely beginnings with the person that I am now. I knew no one, did not know where to look for
5   lodging,[1] and my clothes were dirty. I was very tired and very hungry. I had very little money, but I gave some of it to the people of the boat. At first they refused because I had helped to row the boat, but I insisted. A man is sometimes more generous when he has very little money than when he has plenty, perhaps through fear of being
10   thought to have only a little.

I bought three pennies worth of bread and received three great puffy rolls. I ate one, drank some river water, and gave the other two to a woman and a child who had been in the boat with me.

Feeling much better, I followed some people to a Quaker[2] meeting-
15   house. I was so tired that I fell fast asleep. After the meeting someone was kind enough to wake me up. And so that was the first house I was in, or slept in, in Philadelphia. . . .

Arriving at Moral Perfection

It was about this time I took on the bold project of arriving at moral[3]
20   perfection. I wished to live without committing any fault at any time. I thought I knew right from wrong, and I could not see why I might not always do the one and avoid the other. But the task was more difficult than I had imagined. Sometimes, in resisting one fault, I was surprised by another. I realized that just wanting to be virtuous[4] was
25   not enough, and so I created the following method.

I made a list of thirteen virtues[5] that I believed to be necessary or desirable. They were:

---

1. **lodging** (LOJ ihng): a place to live for a short time.
2. **Quaker** (KWAY kuhr): religious group, also called the Society of Friends.
3. **moral** (MAWR uhl): based on principles of right conduct, rather than law or custom.
4. **virtuous** (VUR chu uhs): good.
5. **virtues** (VUR chooz): particularly good qualities.

1. **Temperance.** Do not eat or drink too much.

2. **Silence.** Speak only what may help others or yourself; avoid silly conversation.

3. **Order.** Let everything have its own place; let each activity have its own time.

4. **Resolution.** Plan to do what you should, and do what you plan to do.

5. **Frugality.** Spend no money except to do good to others or yourself; waste nothing.

6. **Industry.** Do not waste time; do useful things, do nothing unnecessary.

7. **Sincerity.** Do not be dishonest; think and speak innocently and justly.

8. **Justice.** Do not cause harm or fail to help others.

9. **Moderation.** Avoid extremes; do not resent injuries too much.

10. **Cleanliness.** Do not put up with uncleanliness.

11. **Tranquility.** Do not be disturbed by small things or unavoidable accidents.

12. **Chastity.** Do not use sex out of weakness or in ways that could injure your own or another's comfort or reputation.

13. **Humility.** Imitate Jesus[6] and Socrates.[7]

I wanted to make all these virtues into personal habits, so I tried to master them one at a time. I put them in the order that made the most sense, and then I made a little book, in which I allotted a page for each of the virtues. On each page I marked seven columns, one for each day of the week. I crossed these columns with thirteen red lines, marking the beginning of each line with the first letter of one of the virtues. In the proper column, I marked a little black spot every time I found fault with myself. I paid attention to each virtue for a week,

---

6. **Jesus:** great religious leader. The Christian religion was founded on his life and teachings.
7. **Socrates** (SAHK ruh teez): Greek philosopher and teacher.

MAKING INFERENCES

Look over Franklin's list of virtues. Do you think he listed them in order of importance, with No. 1 being the most important? Why or why not? What virtue would you add to or take away from the list?

_____

_____

_____

_____

_____

_____

_____

Here's **HOW**

VOCABULARY

I do not know what *temperance* (line 28) means, but the words following it tell me it probably means "not eating or drinking a lot." The dictionary shows I am right.

VOCABULARY

For any of the virtues in Franklin's list whose meaning you do not know, look for clues in the instructions following each virtue. Then, check a dictionary to see if you got it right.

Here's HOW

MAKING INFERENCES

Looking at the form of the pages that Franklin put in his little book, I think he was very methodical and well organized. The graph would be easy to use.

Your TURN

MAKING INFERENCES

Re-read the last two lines. What does Franklin's plan reveal about his character?

_____

_____

_____

_____

_____

_____

_____

and I went on to the next when I could go a whole week without a black spot. Like a man with a large garden to weed, I knew I could not get rid of all my faults at once.

Form of the Pages

Temperance							
Eat not to dullness. Drink not to elevation.							
	S	M	T	W	T	F	S
T							
S							
O							
R							
F							
I							
S							
J							
M							
Cl							
T							
Ch							
H							

I decided to work on each virtue for a week, taking them in order. I hoped, at the end of thirteen weeks, to see a clean book.

First-Person Point of View

In the left-hand side of the chart below are quotations from the selection. All of these are written using the **first-person point of view.** Rewrite the excerpts from a modern outsider's point of view—such as a reporter or a biographer. (A biographer writes the story of another person's life.) The first-person pronouns *I, me,* and *my* must be changed to *he, Franklin, him,* or *his.* One has been done for you.

Franklin's Original First-Person Narrative	Reporter's or Biographer's Version
1. "I wished to live without committing any fault at any time. . . . But the task was more difficult than I had imagined." (lines 20–23)	
2. "Sometimes, in resisting one fault, I was surprised by another." (lines 23–24)	
3. "In the proper column, I marked a little black spot every time I found fault with myself." (lines 55–56)	In the proper column, Franklin marked a little black spot every time he found fault with himself.
4. "Like a man with a large garden to weed, I knew I could not get rid of all my faults at once." (lines 58–59)	

Speech to the Virginia Convention

Literary Focus: Persuasion

Persuasion is a kind of argument that uses **logic** and **emotion** to convince people to think or act in a certain way. You see and hear many examples of **persuasion** every day. Politicians want people to vote for them. Companies create ads to get you to buy their shampoos, eat at their restaurants, or use their cell-phone services. Sometimes, you are the person trying to persuade someone: "If I mow the lawn, can I go to the concert?"

Reading Skill: Recognizing Modes of Persuasion

It's important to be able to recognize methods of persuasion because you hear so many persuasive appeals every day. A good persuasive speaker or writer appeals to both head and heart, that is, to both **logic** and **emotion.** Appeals to logic are clear, sensible, and based on facts. Appeals to emotion affect the listener's feelings. They attract sympathy to the speaker. The most effective persuasive arguments appeal to both logic and emotion. As you read the speech, decide what kind of persuasive appeals Patrick Henry is making.

Into the Speech

Patrick Henry gave this speech in 1775 to the Virginia House of Burgesses. He was reacting to the words of the previous speakers. These speakers hoped to work out an agreement that did not include independence from Great Britain. Henry wanted to persuade them to change their minds.

Speech to the Virginia Convention

BASED ON THE SPEECH BY **Patrick Henry**

Mr. President:[1] No man thinks more highly than I do of the patriotism and abilities of the worthy gentlemen who have just addressed the House.[2] But I see the subject differently, and I hope you will not think I am disrespectful for speaking my opinions freely.

5 The question before the House is of great importance to this country. It is nothing less than a question of freedom or slavery, and the seriousness of that topic should extend to the freedom of the debate. Only in this way can we arrive at the truth and fulfill our great responsibility to God and our country. It would be disloyal and

10 even treasonous[3] of me to hold back my opinions.

Mr. President, it is natural to hope. We are likely to shut our eyes against a painful truth and be misled till we destroy ourselves. But is this what wise men should do, who are engaged in the struggle for liberty? Are we willing to be people who have eyes, but do not see,

15 and have ears, but do not hear? For my part, I am willing to know the whole truth, to know the worst, and to provide for it.

I am guided by experience and judge the future by the past. And judging by the past, I wish to know what the British government has done in the last ten years to justify the hope these gentlemen

20 speak of. Is it the sly smile with which our petition[4] was received? Do not trust it; it is a trap. Do not let yourselves be betrayed with a kiss.[5] Ask yourselves, how does this gracious reception match their warlike preparations that darken our land? Do fleets and armies contribute to love and peace? Let us not be fooled. These are acts of war, the last

25 arguments that kings use.

What do these preparations mean, if not to make us give in? Can gentlemen see any other possible reason for it? Has Great Britain any enemy, in this part of the world, to make it necessary to have these large armies and navies? No, sir, she has none. They

---

1. **Mr. President:** Henry is addressing the meeting's chairman.
2. **"gentlemen who have just addressed the House":** Henry is referring to the speakers at the Virginia Convention who have just made speeches in favor of accepting the British government's demands.
3. **treasonous** (TREE zuhn uhs): betraying one's country.
4. **petition** (puh TIH shuhn): formal or serious request.
5. **"betrayed with a kiss":** Henry is referring to the Bible story. The apostle Judas betrayed Jesus to the soldiers by identifying him with a kiss.

30 are meant for us and no other. They are sent to put us in the chains
the British government has been making for us. And how can we
oppose them? Shall we try argument? We have been trying that for
ten years. We have nothing new to add. All our arguments have
been useless. Shall we plead with them? What words shall we use
35 that have not already been used? Let us not, I beg you, fool ourselves
any longer.

Sir, we have done all we could to prevent the coming storm. We
have begged the throne of Great Britain to come between us and the
tyranny[6] of the government ministers and Parliament. We have been
40 treated with contempt. We cannot now hope for peace. There is no
longer any room for hope. If we wish to be free, to have those
privileges we have so long fought for, if we do not mean to give up
the noble struggle, we must fight! I repeat it, sir, we must fight! An
appeal to arms and to God is all that is left us!

45 They tell us, sir, that we are weak, that we are unable to fight
so strong an enemy. But when shall we be stronger? Will it be next
week, or next year? Will it be when we are totally disarmed, and
when a British guard is posted in every house? Shall we gather
strength by doing nothing? Shall we resist them by lying down and
50 holding on to false hope, until they tie us hand and foot? Sir, we are
not weak, if we make proper use of the strength that God has given
us. Three million people, armed in the holy cause of liberty, and in
such a country as ours, can triumph over any force sent against us.
Besides, sir, we shall not fight our battles alone. God, who rules the
55 fates of nations, will send us help. Battles, sir, are not won only by
the strong. They are also won by the watchful, the active, the brave.
Besides, sir, we have no choice. It is too late to back down. If we give
up, we will be slaves! The clanking of our chains will be heard
everywhere. War is inevitable[7]—and let it come! I repeat it, sir, let
60 it come!

Here's HOW

VOCABULARY

In line 38, I don't understand why Henry is talking about begging the throne. Why would he beg a fancy chair? Oh, I see. The throne represents the King of England.

Here's HOW

VOCABULARY

I don't know the word *contempt* in line 40. The sentences just before it and just after it suggest that the colonists haven't been treated very well. Henry talks about not having any hope for peace. When I checked in a dictionary, it said *contempt* means "scorn." That makes sense here.

Your TURN

RECOGNIZING PERSUASION

In the paragraph beginning with line 45, Henry asks many questions for the audience to think about. What is the effect of this series of questions on the audience? Write your answer on the lines below.

_____

_____

_____

_____

---

6. **tyranny** (TIHR uh nee): unjust use of power.
7. **inevitable** (ih NEH vuh tuh buhl): certain; sure to happen; can't be avoided.

RECOGNIZING PERSUASION

Henry uses a very strong conclusion to end his speech. What makes Henry's closing lines so persuasive? Write your answer on the lines below.

_____

_____

_____

_____

_____

_____

_____

Gentlemen may cry peace, peace—but there is no peace. The war has actually begun! The next wind that sweeps from the north will bring the clash of battle to our ears! Our brothers are already fighting. Why do we stand idle? Is life so dear, or peace so sweet, as
65 to be purchased at the price of chains and slavery? Forbid it, Almighty God! I know not what course others may take; but as for me, give me liberty, or give me death!

Persuasion

Persuasive writers appeal to the minds and hearts of their audiences. A **logical appeal** uses reasons, facts, and examples to support an idea or claim: "Three fourths of all doctors prefer Tummy Relief for upset stomachs." An **emotional appeal** tugs at people's hearts, hopes, and dreams. "I use Tummy Relief because that's the brand my mother always used." Much persuasive writing is a mixture of logical and emotional appeals.

Below are some quotations from Henry's speech in the left column. The type of appeal is in the right column. Read each quotation. Then, explain the type of appeal on the lines provided. One has already been done for you.

Quotations from Henry's Speech	Type of Appeal
1. "And judging by the past, I wish to know what the British government has done . . . to justify the hope these gentlemen speak of." (lines 18–20)	Mostly logical
2. "They [the large armies and navies] are sent to put us in the chains the British government has been making for us." (lines 30–31)	Mostly emotional
3. "They tell us . . . that we are unable to fight so strong an enemy. But when shall we be stronger?" (lines 45–46)	Mostly logical
4. "We shall not fight our battles alone. God, who rules the fates of nations, will send us help." (lines 54–55) This is an emotional appeal to people's religious faith.	Mostly emotional
5. "I know not what course others may take; but as for me, give me liberty, or give me death!" (lines 66–67)	Mostly emotional

From The Autobiography: The Declaration of Independence

Literary Focus: Parallelism

The repeated use of the same grammatical structure is called **parallelism**. For example, "Give me liberty, or give me death" contains parallel structure. If the sentence had read "Give me liberty or death," the structure would not be parallel.

Parallel	Not Parallel

give me liberty — give me death

give me liberty — death

Thomas Jefferson's use of parallel structure in the Declaration of Independence highlights his arguments and helps him make a powerful plea for independence from English rule.

Reading Skill: Identifying the Main Idea

The **main idea** is the central point a writer is trying to make. As you read, look for the main arguments that support the same idea and the details that support each argument. After you have read this selection, decide what main idea Jefferson is presenting.

Into the Autobiography

Thomas Jefferson worked with four other writers on the Declaration of Independence. The other writers were John Adams, Roger Sherman, Robert Livingston, and Benjamin Franklin. These writers made few changes to Jefferson's first draft. However, Congress insisted on several major adjustments.

This excerpt from Jefferson's autobiography describes the changes Congress wanted. Then it presents the Declaration itself.

The Declaration of Independence

Based on the Autobiography by

Thomas Jefferson

When Congress considered the Declaration of Independence, sections that criticized England were removed because some members believed we had friends in England worth keeping. A section condemning the slave trade was also deleted; South Carolina and Georgia did not want

5 to stop bringing in slaves. Even some congressmen from the North were concerned about this criticism. The debates took up most of three days in July. Finally, every member of the House present, except John Dickinson,[1] approved and signed the document.

A Declaration by the Representatives of the United States of America, in General Congress Assembled

10

Sometimes it is necessary for one group of people to break their political ties with another country. They must take up the separate

15 and equal position to which they are entitled. At such a time they should explain the causes that have led to separation.

We believe that some truths are obvious and clear. First, all men are created equal. God has given them certain inalienable[2] rights, including the rights to life, liberty, and the pursuit of happiness.

20 Governments are formed to protect these rights, and they get their power from the consent of the governed. If a government restricts these rights, the people may change or destroy that government and create a new one. But governments should not be changed for petty causes. Experience has shown that people are more likely to suffer

25 patiently than to rid themselves of an established government. But when there have been many abuses, it is the people's right and duty to throw off that government. The colonies have been patient in their suffering, but now change is necessary. They must get rid of the old government. The king of Great Britain has repeatedly injured us, and

---

1. **John Dickinson** (1732–1808): one of Pennsylvania's representatives to the Congress. He led the conservative opposition to the Declaration and refused to sign it.
2. **inalienable** (in AYL yuh nuh buhl): cannot be given up or taken away.

MAIN IDEA

I think the main idea of the Declaration may be right here in lines 13–16. Sometimes two groups do not get along. Those who disagree should explain why.

MAIN IDEA

In line 17, Jefferson states that some truths are clear. In the following lines he lists these truths. Circle the first truth he mentions.

VOCABULARY

I see a word I don't know in line 23—*petty*. It doesn't have any prefixes that would help me define it. When I re-read the sentence, the author is talking about changing governments. That's a big step. And the author says we shouldn't do it for causes that are petty. I would guess that *petty* means "small" or "unimportant." A check in a dictionary shows that I am right.

30 he has established an absolute tyranny[3] over these states. To prove
this, let the world take a look at the facts.

He has refused to approve laws necessary for the public good.

He has forbidden his governors to pass necessary laws.

He has refused to pass other laws for large districts of people,
35 unless they give up their rights to be represented in the legislature.

He has intentionally called government meetings in inconvenient
locations.

He has dissolved representative groups that opposed his attacks
on the rights of the people.

40 He has refused, after dissolving these groups, to allow new ones
to be elected, thus leaving the people vulnerable to external invasion
and inner conflict.

He has tried to keep people from moving to certain states. He has
opposed laws allowing foreigners to become citizens and made it
45 difficult for them to get land.

He has refused to set up new courts in some states.

He has made our judges dependent on his will.

He has set up many new offices to harass our people and make
them poor.

50 He has kept his armies here in peacetime without the consent of
our legislatures.

He has made military power separate from and superior to civil
power.

He has put us under British Parliament rule and forced us to
55 support large armies. He has cut off our trade with the rest of the
world. He has imposed taxes on us without our consent. He has
deprived us of trial by jury. In some cases he has sent us away to be
tried on invented charges. He has abolished the free system of English
laws in a Canadian province[4] nearby and has established an unfair
60 government there. He has taken away our charters[5] and abolished our
most valuable laws. He has changed our basic forms of government
and stopped our legislatures from meeting.

---

3. **tyranny** (TIHR uh nee): unjust use of authority.
4. **Canadian province:** Québec.
5. **charters:** documents that list the guaranteed rights of a group.

PARALLELISM

In lines 32–72, Jefferson wants
to show that all the items listed
are equal in importance. To
stress this idea, he states each
point in a similar style, making the
ideas parallel.

PARALLELISM

Re-read the sentences
beginning on lines 32, 34, 40,
and 46. Circle the words in
each of the four sentences that
are the same.

MAIN IDEA

Beginning with line 32 and
continuing through line 72,
Jefferson makes some very
strong statements against the
king of England. How could
you summarize the main
argument he is presenting?

_____
_____
_____
_____
_____
_____
_____

PARALLELISM

In lines 65–66, underline the word groups that are parallel in structure.

MAIN IDEA

In lines 77–80, Jefferson has changed his approach a little, but he is still supporting his main idea. First, he listed everything the king had done wrong. Now, he's saying what the colonists did to seek help.

Your TURN

MAIN IDEA

Re-read lines 77–82. List two of the things the colonists did to try to keep peace with England.

_____

_____

_____

_____

_____

_____

_____

_____

_____

_____

_____

He has declared us beyond his protection and waged war against us.

65 He has stolen from our ships, burnt our towns, and destroyed the lives of our people.

He has brought foreign troops here to complete works of death and tyranny that are unworthy of the leader of a civilized nation.

He has taken our citizens captive on the high seas. He has then
70 forced them to bear arms against their country.

He has tried to cause conflict among us and to get the Indians to attack us.

We have asked for justice in the most humble terms. Our repeated requests have been answered by repeated injuries.

75 A king who would do these things is cruel and unfit to rule a free people.

We have not forgotten our British brothers. We have reminded them of the circumstances of our arrival and settlement here. We have appealed to their justice and nobility and to our common ties of
80 family. We have asked for their help, but they have been deaf to the voice of justice. We must therefore consider them the way we consider other nations: as enemies in war and as friends in peace.

We, therefore, the representatives of the United States of America, appealing to God, declare that these colonies are free and independent
85 states. They no longer owe loyalty to the British crown. All political connections between the colonies and Great Britain are dissolved. As free and independent states, they have the power to make war or peace, to form alliances, to establish trade, and to do all other acts and things that independent states do.

90 And for the support of this declaration, with a firm reliance on God's protection, we promise our lives, our fortunes, and our sacred honor.

This Declaration was signed on paper on the fourth of July and was signed again on parchment[6] on the second of August.

---

6. **parchment** (PAHRCH muhnt): a thin animal skin used to write on.

36 HOLT ADAPTED READER

Copyright © by Holt, Rinehart and Winston. All rights reserved.

Parallelism

Jefferson's use of parallelism creates a stately rhythm in the
Declaration of Independence. This rhythm is somewhat formal,
but it is also a very natural expression of how we speak and think.

Complete the chart below by finding additional examples of
Jefferson's use of parallelism in the Declaration. Note that in parallel
constructions the specific *words* are not necessarily the same, but the
forms are the same. The first item is filled in for you.

First Item in Series	Parallel Item in Same Series
1. "He has refused to approve laws necessary for the public good." (line 32)	"He has refused to pass other laws . . ."
2. "We have not forgotten our British brothers." (line 77)	
3. "they have the power to make war or peace." (lines 87–88)	
4. "we promise our lives. . . ." (line 91)	

American Romanticism 1800–1860

Based on the Student Edition text by Gary Q. Arpin

Almost all stories describe a journey. The Bible, the Greek epics, *The Wonderful Wizard of Oz*—all feature a person or a group of people who set out on a quest. In his *Autobiography,* Benjamin Franklin describes his own personal quest. The young Ben leaves his Boston
5 home and travels to Philadelphia to seek his fortune. In many ways, Franklin's journey is uniquely American. He declares his independence from his family and seeks opportunity in the city. His personal goals are like the goals of eighteenth-century America. Both looked for independence and a brighter future.

10 In 1799, the American writer Charles Brockden Brown described a very different journey to the city. In his novel *Arthur Mervyn,* a young farm boy leaves home for Philadelphia. Instead of finding a place of promise, though, the boy is plunged into a world of disease, decay, corruption, and evil.

15 Franklin's journey is told from a rationalist point of view. For rationalists the city was a place of civilization and opportunity. Brown's tale is told from a Romantic one. For the Romantics the city was a place of immorality and death.

For this reason, the Romantic journey often leads into the
20 countryside. To the Romantics the countryside was a place of independence, morality, and healthful living. Sometimes the journey might be into the mind. For example, the works of Edgar Allan Poe show journeys into the imagination. Either way, the Romantic journey is both a flight *from* something and a flight *to* something.

The Romantic Sensibility: Celebrating Imagination

25 In general, Romantics valued feeling over reason. **Romanticism** was originally a European movement that began in the late 1700s and spread throughout Europe into the 1800s. It came to America slightly later and took somewhat different forms.

30 Romanticism first grew in response to **rationalism.** Rationalism had focused on reason and science and had sparked the Industrial

Revolution. With the Industrial Revolution, however, came filthy cities and terrible working conditions. The Romantics distrusted pure reason and instead turned to the imagination. They claimed that the
35 imagination could see and understand truths that the rational mind could not. The Romantics valued imagination, feeling, and nature over reason, logic, and civilization.

The Romantics valued poetry above all other works of the imagination. They contrasted poetry with science, which they saw as
40 a destroyer of truth. Edgar Allan Poe once called science a "vulture" with wings of "dull realities" that preyed on the hearts of poets.

Romantic Escapism: From Dull Realities to Higher Truths

The Romantics wanted to rise above "dull realities" to find truth and
45 beauty. They did this in two ways. First, they explored exotic settings. These settings are sometimes in the more "natural" past or in locations far from civilization and industry. Other times, they explored supernatural worlds or legends and folk tales.

Second, Romantics tried to reflect on the natural world in order to
50 see truth and beauty. This approach is found in many lyric poems. In these poems a speaker discovers in an ordinary scene or object, such as a flower by a stream or a bird flying overhead, some important, deeply felt understanding about life. Like the Puritans, the Romantics found truth in nature. But rather than finding moral lessons of a
55 biblical nature, the Romantics found a more general feeling of mental and emotional rebirth.

Characteristics of American Romanticism

- values feeling over reason
- places faith in the imagination
60 - shuns civilization and seeks nature
- prefers innocence to sophistication
- fights for the individual's freedom and worth
- trusts past wisdom, not progress
- reflects on nature to gain spiritual wisdom
65 - finds beauty and truth in supernatural or imaginative realms

VOCABULARY

Re-read lines 42–48. On the lines below, write a definition of the word *escapism*. Use the context, or words around *escapism*, to help you understand the word.

_____

_____

_____

- sees poetry as the highest work of the imagination
- is inspired by myth, legend, and folklore.

The American Novel and the Wilderness Experience

During the Romantic Period some American writers imitated English
70 and European models. Others believed that America should develop a
literary style of its own. The great American frontier provided a sense
of unlimited possibilities that was not available in Europe, which had
been settled so long ago. Therefore, the first truly American novels
looked westward. They celebrated the spirit of a growing nation.

75   James Fenimore Cooper (1789–1851) wrote about unique American
settings and characters: frontier communities, American Indians, and
backwoodsmen. Cooper also created the first American hero: Natty
Bumppo. This character's simple morality, love of nature, and almost
superhuman inventiveness make him a true Romantic hero.

80 ## A New Kind of Hero

Most Europeans thought of America as a crude, uncivilized place.
However, Cooper and other Romantic novelists turned the insult on its
head. They suggested that American virtue rested in its innocence.
Truth, they said, could not be found in the libraries or cities of Europe
85 but instead in the wilderness of America.

Ben Franklin represents the rationalist hero. He is worldly,
educated, and civilized. He looks to the city to better himself and
make a brighter future. The typical Romantic hero, however, is
youthful and innocent. He relies on common sense rather than book
90 learning and is close to nature. Because women represented marriage
and civilization (to many male writers), Romantic heroes are often
uncomfortable around them.

Today Americans still create Romantic heroes. Modern-day Natty
Bumppos appear in the form of Superman, Luke Skywalker, and
95 Indiana Jones, and dozens of other western, detective, and fantasy
heroes.

Your TURN

VOCABULARY

The word *backwoodsmen* is in
line 77. Use your knowledge of
the word's parts to write a
definition on the lines below.

_____

_____

_____

_____

_____

Characteristics of the American Romantic Hero

- is youthful and innocent
- has a strong sense of honor
100 • has knowledge that comes from experience, not formal learning
- loves nature and avoids town life
- seeks truth in the natural world

American Romantic Poetry: Read at Every Fireside

The goals of American Romantic poets were different from those of
105 the Romantic novelists. While the novelists looked for new subject
matter, the poets wanted to prove that Americans were not ignorant
hicks. To do this, they wrote poems in a style much like the poems of
England.

Henry Wadsworth Longfellow (1807–1882), John Greenleaf
110 Whittier, Oliver Wendell Holmes, and James Russell Lowell were
known as the Fireside Poets. They were called Fireside Poets because
their poems were often read aloud at the fireside. In their time period,
and for a long time after, they were the most popular poets America
had ever produced.

115 Because they preferred the old, established styles of poetry, the
Fireside Poets were unable to recognize the American poetry of the
future. In 1855, Whittier read the work of a young poet, Walt
Whitman, and promptly threw it into the fire. After reading the same
poetry, the author Ralph Waldo Emerson wrote the young poet a
120 letter. "I greet you," Emerson wrote to Whitman, "at the beginning of
a great career."

The Transcendentalists: True Reality Is Spiritual

Emerson led a group known as the Transcendentalists. These people
believed that to find the truth about God, the universe, and one's self,
125 one must *transcend*, or go beyond, the everyday experiences of the
physical world.

Transcendentalism was not new. It originated in the ancient
Greek philosophy of idealism. Idealists said that true reality was found
in ideas, not in the imperfect physical world. They sought the pure

Here's HOW

VOCABULARY

Fireside is a word I've never heard anyone use. I can figure out, from lines 111–112, that it means the "place at the side of the fire," but most houses nowadays don't have fireplaces, or if they do, families don't spend a lot of time sitting around them reading poetry.

130 reality—the "ideal" that was beneath physical appearances. American Transcendentalists were idealists in a more practical sense. They believed that humanity could be perfected, and they worked to make this ideal a reality.

Emerson and Transcendentalism: The
135 ## American Roots

Through his books and lectures, Emerson became the best-known member of the Transcendentalists. His Transcendentalism added ideas from Europe and Asia to a distinctly American base.

Emerson drew much of his thought from Puritanism. The Puritans
140 believed that God revealed himself through the Bible *and* through the physical world. For example, Jonathan Edwards found God in the sun, moon, and stars. This mystical view of the world was passed on to the American Romantics. It was also passed on to Emerson. "Every natural fact," he wrote, "is a symbol of some spiritual fact."

145 ## Emerson's Optimistic Outlook

Emerson's view of the world came from his intuition, not from logic. Intuition is our ability to know things through feeling rather than reason. Benjamin Franklin, on the other hand, used reason to view the world. Franklin did not gaze on nature and feel the presence of a
150 Divine Soul. Instead, he saw nature as something to be examined scientifically.

Positive thinking, or optimism, guided Emerson. He strongly believed that God is good and that God works through nature. If we trust in our own power to know God directly, Emerson thought, we
155 will see that we, too, are a part of the Divine Soul.

Emerson's optimism appealed to people who lived in a time full of worries—worries about money, about slavery, about the future of the nation. Emerson gave them a comforting message. If the world depresses you, he suggested, look within yourself. The God within
160 will connect you to the peace and beauty of the universe.

Here's HOW

VOCABULARY

The word *mystical* (line 142) sounds as if it might be related to *mystery*, but I'd better look it up. The dictionary tells me it means "relating to spiritual feelings or ideas."

A Transcendental View of the World

- Everything, including people, is a reflection of the divine.

- The physical world is a doorway to the spiritual world.

- People can use intuition to sense God in nature or in their
165 own souls.

- A person is his or her own best authority.

- Feeling and intuition are superior to reason and intellect.

The Dark Romantics

Not all writers and thinkers of the time agreed with the idealistic
170 Transcendentalists. Nathaniel Hawthorne, Herman Melville, and Edgar
Allan Poe are known as the Dark Romantics. Because of their gloomy
view of the world, some people see these writers as anti-
Transcendentalists. But the Dark Romantics had much in common
with Emerson and his followers. Both groups valued feeling over
175 reason. Both groups saw the events of the world as signs or symbols
that pointed beyond.

However, the Dark Romantics did not agree with the optimism of
the Transcendentalists. They thought that Emerson took only the
bright side of Puritanism and ignored its belief in the wickedness of
180 humanity. To create a greater balance, the Dark Romantics explored
both good *and* evil. They looked at the effects of guilt and sin on the
mind and soul, including madness. Behind the pasteboard masks of
polite society, they saw the horror of evil. From this vision the Dark
Romantics shaped a new, truly American literature.

VOCABULARY

Use context clues and your knowledge of the two parts of the word *pasteboard* (line 182) to write a definition below.

_____

_____

_____

_____

_____

_____

_____

Thanatopsis

Literary Focus: Theme

The **theme** of a poem is what the poet is saying about life. Usually, poets don't state their themes directly. Instead, you have to think about what all the words, images, and figures of speech say to you. Then you can see the theme. The subject of "Thanatopsis" is what happens to people when they die. What the poem says about this subject is its theme.

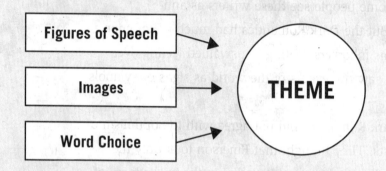

Reading Skill: Reading Inverted Sentences

William Cullen Bryant often makes use of **inversion**—a rearrangement of the usual word order in sentences. The usual order of words in English sentences is subject, then verb, and then object. *Reika kicked the ball.* An inverted order might be *The ball Reika kicked.* If you have trouble understanding sentences in the poem, try rearranging the words.

Into the Poem

William Cullen Bryant was in his late teens when he wrote his first draft of "Thanatopsis." He was looking for answers to how to accept death. He finds his answers in nature. He observes that when we die we become part of nature, along with everyone who has already died and everyone who will die.

Thanatopsis

William Cullen Bryant

William Cullen Bryant was a Romantic poet. In his time that title did not refer to a person who writes poetry about love. Instead, it referred to a poet who shows an emotional response to life. Romantic poets placed feeling above thought. They valued poetry above science and rural life above city life. They believed that studying nature outdoors could bring as much truth to humans as doing scientific experiments. "Thanatopsis" is a nature poem in which Bryant presents his view (*opsis*, in Greek) of death (*thanatos*).

The poetic form that Bryant uses is called **blank verse**. If you look at the lines of the poem, you will see that the lines do not rhyme. However, most lines have the same number of syllables and a regular rhythm.

To him who in the love of Nature holds
Communion with her visible forms, she speaks
A various language; for his gayer hours
She has a voice of gladness, and a smile
5   And eloquence of beauty, and she glides
Into his darker musings, with a mild
And healing sympathy, that steals away
Their sharpness, ere[1] he is aware. When thoughts
Of the last bitter hour come like a blight
10 Over thy spirit, and sad images
Of the stern agony, and shroud, and pall,[2]
And breathless darkness, and the narrow house,[3]
Make thee to shudder, and grow sick at heart;—
Go forth, under the open sky, and list[4]
15 To Nature's teachings, while from all around—

---

1. ere (ayr): before.
2. pall (pawl): coffin cover.
3. narrow house: grave.
4. list: listen.

Earth and her waters, and the depths of air—
Comes a still voice.—

IN OTHER WORDS A person who studies Nature learns that she can share and reflect his or her happiness. She can also offer sympathy in times of pain, sorrow, and death. A person who thinks about death should look to Nature to find answers.

Yet[5] a few days, and thee
The all-beholding sun shall see no more
In all his course; nor yet in the cold ground,
20 Where thy pale form was laid, with many tears,
Nor in the embrace of ocean, shall exist
Thy image. Earth, that nourished thee, shall claim
Thy growth, to be resolved to earth again,
And, lost each human trace, surrendering up
25 Thine individual being, shalt thou go
To mix forever with the elements,
To be a brother to the insensible rock
And to the sluggish clod,[6] which the rude swain[7]
Turns with his share,[8] and treads upon. The oak
30 Shall send his roots abroad, and pierce thy mold.

IN OTHER WORDS Soon you will die and the sun will no longer be able to see you. No image of you will exist in the earth or ocean. But your dead body will join with Nature. You will be buried in the ground, and become part of the earth and rocks, and trees will grow in you.

Yet not to thine eternal resting place
Shalt thou retire alone, nor couldst thou wish

---

5. **Yet . . . :** Here, the voice of Nature begins to speak.
6. **sluggish clod:** lump of dirt, which lacks energy.
7. **rude swain:** uneducated country youth.
8. **share:** short for "plowshare."

THANATOPSIS **47**

Your
TURN

READING INVERTED SENTENCES

Lines 17–18 contain an inversion. In the lines below, rearrange the words into the usual English sentence order. (Remember that *thee* means "you.")

_____

_____

_____

_____

_____

Your
TURN

THEME

Nature tells the speaker what happens to the bodies of humans when they die. Underline words in lines 22–30 that support the theme that the dead become part of Nature.

Here's
HOW

VOCABULARY

In the word *insensible* (line 27) I see the word *sense.* I know the prefix *in–* means "without" or "not." I guess *insensible* means "without sense." I'll check in a dictionary to make sure. Yes, my guess was correct. Oh, *sense* here means "feeling" rather than "ability to reason," so *insensible* means "without feeling."

Your TURN

VOCABULARY

What does the word *vales* in line 38 mean? Use context clues to help you figure out its meaning. Then, write your definition on the lines below.

_____

_____

Here's HOW

THEME

An earlier theme in the poem was: *When we die, we become part of nature.* I think the same theme is here in lines 37–45, when the poet says the whole beautiful earth is a magnificent tomb for human beings.

Your TURN

THEME

Lines 58–72 say that we aren't alone when we die because everyone who has ever lived also dies. Do you find this thought comforting? Explain.

_____

_____

_____

_____

_____

Couch more magnificent. Thou shalt lie down

With patriarchs of the infant world—with kings,

35 The powerful of the earth—the wise, the good,

Fair forms, and hoary seers[9] of ages past,

All in one mighty sepulcher.[10] The hills

Rock-ribbed and ancient as the sun,—the vales

Stretching in pensive quietness between;

40 The venerable woods—rivers that move

In majesty, and the complaining brooks

That make the meadows green; and, poured round all,

Old Ocean's gray and melancholy waste,—

Are but the solemn decorations all

45 Of the great tomb of man. The golden sun,

The planets, all the infinite host of heaven,

Are shining on the sad abodes of death,

Through the still lapse of ages. All that tread

The globe are but a handful to the tribes

50 That slumber in its bosom.—Take the wings

Of morning,[11] pierce the Barcan wilderness,[12]

Or lose thyself in the continuous woods

Where rolls the Oregon,[13] and hears no sound,

Save his own dashings—yet the dead are there:

55 And millions in those solitudes, since first

The flight of years began, have laid them down

In their last sleep—the dead reign there alone.

So shalt thou rest, and what if thou withdraw

In silence from the living, and no friend

60 Take note of thy departure? All that breathe

Will share thy destiny. The gay will laugh

When thou art gone, the solemn brood of care

Plod on, and each one as before will chase

His favorite phantom; yet all these shall leave

---

9. **hoary seers:** white-haired prophets.
10. **sepulcher** (SEH puhl kuhr): burial place.
11. **Take . . . morning:** allusion to Psalm 139:9: "If I take the wings of the morning . . ."
12. **Barcan wilderness:** desert near Barca (now al-Marj), Libya, in North Africa.
13. **Oregon:** early name for the Columbia River, which flows between Washington and Oregon.

65 Their mirth and their employments, and shall come
And make their bed with thee. As the long train
Of ages glides away, the sons of men,
The youth in life's fresh spring, and he who goes
In the full strength of years, matron and maid,
70 The speechless babe, and the gray-headed man—
Shall one by one be gathered to thy side,
By those, who in their turn shall follow them.

IN OTHER WORDS You will not go alone to the grave. You will be with the greatest people in history—kings, men of power. Those who were wise, good, and beautiful are all buried together. The rocky hills; the quiet valleys; the ancient forests; rivers, brooks, and oceans—all are simply decorations for the great tomb of humanity. The sun, the planets, and all the heavenly bodies look down on this place of death. All those who walk on the earth are just a handful compared to the number of dead people who are buried in it. The dead are everywhere in nature. The newly dead join together with generations of people who have gone before them. No one really dies alone. The living will keep on with their joys and worries, but they will join the dead someday.

So[14] live, that when thy summons comes to join
The innumerable caravan, which moves
75 To that mysterious realm, where each shall take
His chamber in the silent halls of death,
Thou go not, like the quarry slave at night,
Scourged[15] to his dungeon, but, sustained and soothed
By an unfaltering trust, approach thy grave,
80 Like one who wraps the drapery of his couch
About him, and lies down to pleasant dreams.

Your TURN

THEME

In lines 73–81, the poet sums up his ideas about how to live. Write in your own words what you think he is advising.

14. **So . . . :** The speaker's voice resumes here.
15. **Scourged** (SKOORG'D): whipped.

IN OTHER WORDS The original speaker returns. He advises people to live in such a way that, when they die, they will not meet death with dread like a person whipped and held in slavery. Instead, they will approach death as if going to bed to enjoy pleasant dreams.

Theme Chart

The **theme** of a poem or other literary work is the insight it offers into human experience. To figure out the overall theme of "Thanatopsis," first figure out the themes of its parts. Write your ideas in the boxes below. Two have been done for you. Then, think about their meanings to come up with the overall theme.

Themes in "Thanatopsis"

Lines 1–17 We can learn a lot from nature.
Lines 17–30
Lines 31–57
Lines 58–72 You do not die alone; everyone who has lived dies.
Lines 73–81
Overall Theme

From Self-Reliance

Literary Focus: Figures of Speech—Metaphor

A **metaphor** is a common figure of speech you probably use every day. Metaphors are imaginative comparisons of unlike things that are not meant to be taken literally but that increase our understanding of what is being described. For instance, when you say someone is hard-hearted, you do not mean that his heart has turned to rock but rather that he has no feelings or is unsympathetic. Here is another example:

Literal Meaning
Her heart is made of shiny metal.

Metaphor
Her heart is made of gold.

Metaphoric Meaning
She is kind and loving.

Reading Skill: Understanding Figures of Speech—Metaphors

A good metaphor uses a characteristic of one thing to help us see something else in a new way. When you come across a metaphor, ask yourself, "What do these two things have in common?" and "What is the writer trying to tell me by this comparison?"

Into the Essay

Ralph Waldo Emerson was a very popular writer and speaker in the decades before the Civil War. His message of the right of each person to chart his or her own path was what the citizens of this new, young nation wanted to hear. In "Self-Reliance," Emerson advises readers not to conform to what society says but to "trust yourself." As you read the essay, think about the meaning of *self-reliance.* How is this word different from *selfishness*?

FROM

Self-Reliance

BASED ON THE ESSAY BY

Ralph Waldo Emerson

Here's HOW

UNDERSTANDING METAPHORS

When Ralph Waldo Emerson says "imitation is suicide" (line 2), he is using a metaphor. I think he means that imitating other people is like killing our spirit—not killing our bodies.

Your TURN

UNDERSTANDING METAPHORS

Emerson compares the idea "Trust in yourself" to an iron string that people's hearts vibrate to (line 14). Describe what you think this metaphor means.

_____

_____

_____

_____

Your TURN

UNDERSTANDING METAPHORS

Circle the metaphor in line 28. Then, describe the comparison on the lines below.

_____

_____

_____

_____

There is a time in every man's education when he realizes that it is foolish to envy others and that imitation is suicide. He understands that he must accept himself exactly as he is. He sees that, although the wide universe is full of good, he will not receive one kernel of

5 nourishing corn unless he tills the plot of ground given to him. The power in each man is unique, and only he knows what he can do. Each sees the world differently, and each remembers in his own special way. Each man must express his own individuality. We only half express ourselves, and are ashamed of that divine idea which

10 each of us represents. A man is happy when he has put his heart and soul into his work and done his best. If he speaks or acts otherwise, he has no peace. His genius deserts him, and he has no new ideas, no hope.

Trust yourself. Every heart vibrates to that iron string. Accept

15 the place God has found for you. Accept your companions and the events of your life. The great have always done so, trusting the feelings of their hearts and the work of their hands. We must all accept this destiny and not hide in some corner like children, invalids, or cowards. We must do good, obey the will of God, and advance on

20 Chaos and the Dark. . . .

These are the voices we hear in solitude, but they become weak as we enter into the world. Society discourages the manhood of every one of its members. It is like a joint-stock company. The members of society agree to surrender their freedom and individuality in exchange

25 for security. They try to conform, to be the same. Self-reliance is not popular, because conformity does not love truth and creativity.

Anyone who wants to be a strong individual must be a nonconformist. That is, he must not blindly accept society's beliefs and customs. He who wishes to be great must discover for himself

30 what goodness means and not be held back by society's constraints. Nothing is more sacred than the integrity of your own mind. Be true to yourself, and the world will applaud you. . . .

A foolish consistency is the hobgoblin of little minds. A great soul has simply nothing to do with consistency. He may just as well
35 concern himself with his shadow on the wall. Speak clearly what you think today, and speak your truth tomorrow, even if it is different from today's. You may be misunderstood, but is it so bad to be misunderstood? Pythagoras was misunderstood, and Socrates, and Jesus, and Luther, and Copernicus, and Galileo, and Newton,° and
40 every pure and wise spirit. To be great is to be misunderstood. . . .

UNDERSTANDING METAPHORS

Emerson compares consistency to a "hobgoblin of little minds" (line 33). The dictionary tells me that a *hobgoblin* is something frightening that is not really there. Since Emerson says in the next sentence that a great soul has "nothing to do with consistency" (line 34), I guess the metaphor means that small-minded people are scared into always being consistent—that is, always behaving and thinking in the same way.

° **Pythagoras . . . Newton:** Famous men whose ideas were not accepted at first. Pythagoras (c. 580–500 B.C.) and Socrates (c. 470–399 B.C.) were Greek philosophers. Jesus (c. 6 B.C.– 30 A.D.) was the founder of Christianity. Luther (1483–1546) was the leader of the Protestant Reformation in Germany. Copernicus (1473–1543) was a Polish astronomer; Galileo (1564–1642) was an Italian astronomer; and Newton (1642–1727) was an English mathematician.

Metaphor

Emerson makes some of his points by using **metaphors** that compare abstract ideas to ordinary things. To sharpen your understanding of metaphors, complete the following chart. The left-hand column lists some of Emerson's metaphors. In the right-hand column, explain the meaning of the metaphors in your own words. One has been done for you.

Emerson's Metaphors	Metaphoric Meaning
1. "imitation is suicide" (line 2)	
2. "Trust yourself. Every heart vibrates to that iron string." (line 14)	
3. "Society . . . is like a joint-stock company" (lines 22–23)	Every member of a society has a share of the responsibilities and will receive a share of benefits.
4. "A foolish consistency is the hobgoblin of little minds." (line 33)	

Vocabulary Development

Developing Vocabulary

You really *own* a word when you can use it in your own writing. To be sure you understand the meanings of some important words from "Self-Reliance," read each definition below carefully. Then, use each word in a sentence of your own. One has been done for you.

1. self-reliance (title and line 25): trust in or dependence on one's own ideas or abilities.

My sentence: _____

_____

_____

2. individuality (line 8): all the qualities that make one person different from others.

My sentence: _____

_____

_____

3. conformity (line 26): behavior that follows established rules and customs.

My sentence: _____

_____

_____

4. constraints (line 30): restrictions; things that hold back by force.

My sentence: _____

_____

_____

5. integrity (line 31): uprightness, honesty, and sincerity.

My sentence: The students elected Alex class president because they admired his integrity.

_____

From Resistance to Civil Government

Literary Focus: Paradox

A **paradox** is a statement that seems to contradict itself but is also somehow true. A good example is Juliet's words from Shakespeare's *The Tragedy of Romeo and Juliet*. As she leaves her lover Romeo, Juliet says, "Good night, good night! Parting is such sweet sorrow. . . ."

Sweet: I am with you, the person I love. That makes me happy

Paradox
Sweet Sorrow

Sorrow: I have to leave you. That makes me sad.

Reading Skill: Asking Questions

When someone says something you don't understand, what do you do? You ask questions and listen to the answers until you do understand. Do the same with this essay. By questioning what you read, you will more easily see the conflict and also the truth, within the paradox of civil disobedience.

Into the Essay

In 1846, the United States declared war on Mexico. Henry David Thoreau thought the war was unjustified, so he refused to pay a tax that would support the war. He was jailed for his refusal. This act was the basis for his essay, which has also been titled "Civil Disobedience." Many people, including Martin Luther King, Jr., and Mohandas K. Gandhi, view Thoreau's idea of civil disobedience as an important part of citizenship. What do you think? Let Thoreau's essay help you decide.

FROM **Resistance to Civil Government**

BASED ON THE ESSAY BY

Henry David Thoreau

PARADOX

In the quotation in lines 2–3, there are two opposite ideas: 1) the job of the government is to govern, 2) the best government does not govern at all. I can't see how this would work. I will have to read on and see what truth Thoreau is trying to get across in this paradox.

ASKING QUESTIONS

In line 24, Thoreau says that his only duty is to do what he thinks is right. How can everyone do that? What if what I think is right is the opposite of what someone else thinks is right?

PARADOX

Thoreau sees a paradox in his neighbors' behavior. What contradiction does he describe in lines 27–29?

_____

_____

_____

_____

_____

I heartily accept the motto—"That government is best which governs least"[1]—and I would like to see it carried out. I also believe that "That government is best which governs not at all." People are not yet ready for that kind of government. Government at best is but a means to an

5 end, but government often does not work well to achieve that end.

The objection to a standing army[2] can also be applied to a standing government. Both can easily be put to wrong use. The present Mexican war is an example of this. It is the work of only a few people using the government for their own gain.

10 The American government does not keep the country free—the people do that. It does not settle the West or educate. It is the American people who have done all these good things. They might have done even more if the government had gotten out of the way.

But to speak practically and as a citizen, I do not ask for no

15 government right now; rather, I ask for better government *at once*. Every person should describe what kind of government he or she could respect, and that will be a step toward getting it.

After all, the majority rules not because they are right, but because they are stronger than the minority. But a government based

20 always on majority rule cannot be based on justice. Can there not be a government where conscience decides right and wrong? I think we should be individuals first and people ruled by a government second. We should work for respect for what is right rather than for the law. The only duty I have is to do what I think is right.

25 It is not a man's duty to get rid of a wrong, but at least he should avoid supporting it. This means that I cannot go after my goals if they harm someone else. Now, some of my neighbors say they will not support slavery or go off to fight against Mexico. But they help these causes with their tax money. If we refuse to help an unjust cause, we

30 should not have to support an unjust government that promotes that cause.

I meet the government face to face once a year when the tax collector comes to see me. By refusing to pay my taxes to this person,

---

1. **"That . . . least":** This statement has been attributed to Thomas Jefferson.
2. **standing army:** an army that is kept going permanently, in times of peace as well as in times of war.

I go against the government's authority. I then watch to see how the tax collector treats me. He must choose whether to treat me respectfully, as a neighbor, or as a madman and a disturber of the peace. I believe that if only one honest person in the state of Massachusetts refused to own slaves and refused to give money to a government that allows slavery, it would be the end of slavery in America. It does not matter how small a beginning may be: What is once well done is done forever.

I have paid no poll tax[3] for six years. For this reason, I once spent a night in jail. As I stood looking at the thick stone walls and the iron bars, I thought how foolish the government was to lock me up. Yes, there was a wall of stone between me and my townsmen. However, my fellow townsmen would have to break through an even thicker wall before they could be as free as I was. They could imprison my body but not my mind. I felt as if I alone of all my townsmen had paid my tax. I saw that the government was really weak, and I lost all remaining respect for it and pitied it.

My night in prison was interesting. My cellmate was a pleasant fellow, and when the door was locked he showed me where to hang my hat. He was there, he told me, because he was accused of burning a barn. He insisted it was an accident, and I believed him because he seemed an honest fellow. He had been there three months waiting for his trial. Still, he was well fed and content.

He looked out one window and I looked out the other, realizing that in jail the main thing to do was look out the window. My fellow prisoner told me stories about some of the men who had been locked up in the cell. These stories had never been heard outside these walls. At last we said good night and blew out the lamp.

Lying there for one night was like being in a far country. I listened to the evening sounds of the village as I never had before. It gave me a different impression of my native town. I began to understand what the people who lived there were like.

In the morning they gave us our breakfast, and my cellmate went out to work in a field. He told me he did not think that he would ever see me again.

---

3. **poll tax:** fee some states and localities required from each citizen as a qualification for voting. It is now considered unconstitutional in the United States to charge such a tax.

Your TURN

ASKING QUESTIONS

In lines 37–41, Thoreau argues that the principled action of only one person can change society's institutions. What questions would you ask about this idea?

_____

_____

_____

_____

_____

_____

_____

_____

Here's HOW

PARADOX

In lines 43–48, Thoreau says he does not feel locked up, although he is in prison. He says his body is in prison but his thoughts and imagination are free—unlike those of his fellow citizens. I think the bigger truth here is that no one can lock up your mind, except yourself.

RESISTANCE TO CIVIL GOVERNMENT   **61**

He was right. Someone paid my tax, even though I did not want them to, and I walked free. I saw my town, my state, and my country in a new way. I saw how far I could trust my fellow villagers to be my friends. They ran no risks. They did not live and act on any principle. They were very different from me. They thought they would save their souls by saying a few prayers and walking a straight but useless path. I believe that most of them did not even know there was a jail in the village.

I went about my business, going to get a shoe I had left to be repaired. I then joined some people for a berry-picking party. We went high up in the hills, and the government was nowhere to be seen.

And that is the story of "My Prisons."

The government is fair and just only when it has the support and agreement of its citizens. It can have no power over me and my property that I do not allow it to have. The progress from a monarchy—being ruled by a king—to a democracy is progress toward a true respect for the individual person. But any government must see the individual as the true source of its power and treat each person in that way. I imagine a government that would be fair to all men. I imagine a government that would treat the individual with respect. I imagine a government tolerant of those who live apart from society, yet who still fulfill their neighborly duties. This kind of government would prepare the way for a still more perfect and glorious state. I have imagined such a government, but I have not yet seen it anywhere.

Paradox

A **paradox** is a statement that seems to contradict itself but is also somehow true. Paradox was one of Thoreau's favorite literary devices. The idea that a contradiction can contain a truth is in itself paradoxical—and truthful.

The first column of the chart below contains paradoxical statements from the selection. The second column is for one side of the paradox. The third column is for the other side of the paradox. The last column is for the truth revealed by the paradox. Some sections of the chart have been filled in. See if you can fill in the other sections.

Paradoxical Statement	One Side of the Paradox	Other Side of the Paradox	Truth of the Paradox
1. "My fellow townsmen would have to break through an even thicker wall before they could be as free as I was."	Thoreau was in jail; the other towns-men were free.		Freedom of the mind has nothing to do with freedom of the body.
2. "That government is best which governs least."		The best govern-ment is one that does little governing.	Government should give people room for doing what they think is right.
3. "I felt as if I alone of all my townsmen had paid my tax."	Thoreau did not pay the tax.		Thoreau felt that he had contributed most to society because he had acted in a moral way by not giving money to support things he thought were wrong.

The Minister's Black Veil

Literary Focus: Symbol

A **symbol** is something that has meaning in itself but also stands for something more than itself. You've seen the dove used as a symbol of peace. Uncle Sam symbolizes the United States, and the four-leaf clover is a symbol of luck. What other symbols can you think of?

Reading Skill: Making Inferences

When you make an **inference** about a character or event, you are making an educated guess. This guess is based on clues in the text and on your own knowledge and experience. You make inferences in everyday life too. For example, your neighbor gets a new puppy. How would you infer what your neighbor is feeling?

My Experience

I would love to have a puppy.

Clue I Observe

I see my neighbor playing with the puppy and laughing.

Inference

My neighbor is very happy.

Into the Short Story

This story is set in a New England town during Puritan times. It is about a young minister who shocks his congregation by wearing a black veil over his face when he preaches the Sunday sermon. The minister won't say why he is wearing the veil, and he won't take it off. The veil affects characters in the story in different ways. The story looks at how the veil affects the minister's congregation, his social standing, his relationship with his fiancée, and his entire life.

Nathaniel Hawthorne

The Minister's Black Veil

A Parable

On a bright Sunday morning the good people of Milford were on their way to church. They paused outside and waited for their minister to appear. When they saw him walking slowly along the road, they were startled to see that he wore a black veil over his face.

5   On a nearer view the veil seemed to be two folds of crape,[1] which entirely covered his features except for the mouth and chin. He must have been able to see through it, however, because he walked with a steady pace and nodded to some of the people.

"I can't really feel our good Mr. Hooper's face is behind that piece
10 of cloth," said one man.

"I don't like it," muttered an old woman. "He has changed himself into something awful by hiding his face."

"Our parson has gone mad!" cried Goodman[2] Gray, following the minister into the meetinghouse.

15   There was a general bustle when the minister entered, and everyone stared at him. He approached the pulpit and stood face to face with his congregation, except for the black veil. The veil shook with his breath as he gave out the psalm, read the Scriptures, and looked up to God in prayer. Was the minister trying to hide his face
20 from God as he prayed?

A few people were so upset they had to leave. Perhaps the faces of the congregation were as fearful to the minister as his black veil was to them.

Mr. Hooper was a good preacher, though his method was mildly
25 persuasive rather than thunderous. He spoke softly now of the secret sins that lie in the hearts of all people, those we hide from our nearest and dearest and even try to hide from ourselves. Every listener, even the most innocent, felt that the preacher had crept up on them and discovered their hidden sins.

---

1. **crape** (krayp): a kind of black cloth worn as a sign of mourning.
2. **Goodman:** form of polite address similar to *Mister.*

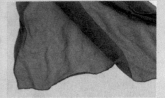

30　After the service the people rushed from the church in confusion. They noticed that they felt better when they lost sight of the black veil. Some whispered together, but others went home in silent thought. Others talked and laughed loudly. Some believed they could figure out the mystery. Others said there was no mystery at all,

35　but only that the minister's eyes were weak and needed to be shaded from the light.

The minister treated everyone with his usual kindness and respect. No one competed for the honor of walking beside him, however, and old Squire[3] Saunders forgot to invite him home for

40　dinner as he usually did. As the minister returned to the parsonage, he noticed all the people staring at him, and a sad smile gleamed faintly from beneath the veil.

"How strange," said a lady, "that a simple black veil should become such a terrible thing on Mr. Hooper's face!"

45　"Something must be wrong with his mind," said her husband, the town doctor. "That simple veil makes him seem like a ghost."

"I would not be alone with him for the world," said the lady. "I wonder he is not afraid to be alone with himself!"

"Men sometimes are so," said her husband.

50　The minister presided that afternoon at the funeral of a young lady. Here his black veil seemed appropriate. As he bent over the dead young woman, it seemed that he held the veil so that even she could not see his face. Mr. Hooper gave a tender prayer, full of heartbreak and sorrow and yet filled with divine hope. The people

55　trembled when he prayed that everyone might be ready, as he trusted this young maiden had been, for the dreadful hour that would snatch away the veil from their faces. After the funeral the mourners proceeded to the graveyard with Mr. Hooper following. It seemed to some, as they looked back, that the minister and the dead girl's spirit

60　were walking hand in hand behind the procession.

---

3. **Squire:** a gentleman; the main landowner of a village.

Here's HOW

VOCABULARY

The word *parsonage* in line 40 looks familiar. I recognize the root word *parson* as meaning a "minister," so I would guess the parsonage is the minister's home. I checked a dictionary, and I was right.

Your TURN

VOCABULARY

Use context clues in the surrounding sentence to figure out what *presided* (line 50) means. Write your answer on the lines below.

_____

_____

Your TURN

SYMBOL

In lines 54–57, what veil do you think Mr. Hooper is referring to? Write your answer on the lines below.

_____

_____

_____

_____

That evening, the handsomest couple in Milford village were to be married. The guests at the wedding awaited the minister's arrival with impatience. When Mr. Hooper came, the first thing that their eyes rested on was the same horrible black veil, which had added

65 deeper gloom to the funeral and could mean nothing but evil to the wedding. Everyone felt as though a dark cloud had settled over the joyous occasion. As the minister raised a toast to the couple, he caught a glimpse of himself in the mirror. He himself was now horrified at the sight of the black veil. He shuddered—his lips grew

70 white—and spilled the wine upon the carpet. Then he rushed out into the night where the Earth, too, had on her Black Veil.

The next day, everyone in the village spoke of nothing but the black veil. One playful child put a black hanky over his face, frightening both his playmates and himself.

75 Nobody had the courage to ask the minister about the veil, although he had always welcomed people's concerns. Finally, a group was chosen to question him, but once they were in his presence, they were unable to speak. The black veil seemed to hang down over the minister's heart, the symbol of a fearful secret between

80 him and them.

The only person in the village who had courage enough to ask him about the veil was Elizabeth, the young woman he had promised to marry. "There is nothing so terrible in this veil," she said, "except that it hides a face I am glad to look upon. Lay it aside, and tell

85 me why you put it on."

"There is an hour to come," he said, "when all of us shall cast aside our veils. Beloved friend, I will wear this piece of cloth till then. I have vowed to wear it always," he continued. "No mortal eye will see it withdrawn, even you."

90 "What terrible thing has happened to you?" Elizabeth asked.

"It is a sign of mourning," replied Mr. Hooper.

"People will whisper that you hide a secret sin," said Elizabeth.

"If I hide my face for sorrow," he said, "there is reason enough. And if I cover it for secret sin, who might not do the same?"

95 After pleading with him for some time, Elizabeth finally fell silent. The tears rolled down her cheeks. As she looked at him, the terrors of the black veil soon took the place of sorrow. She stood before him, trembling.

"And do you feel it then at last?" he said mournfully.

100 She did not reply but turned and started to leave the room. "Have patience with me," he cried. "It is but a mortal veil—it is not for eternity. Oh! You know not how lonely I am and how frightened to be alone behind my black veil. Do not desert me!"

"Lift the veil just once," said she, "and look me in the face."

105 "Never! It cannot be!" he replied.

"Then, farewell," said Elizabeth, and she left.

From that time no more attempts were made to remove the minister's black veil or to discover the secret it was supposed to hide. But the minister could not walk about with peace of mind. The

110 timid would avoid him, and others would throw themselves purposely in his way. Children ran off when they saw him coming. He gave up his usual walk at sunset to the burial ground, for there were always faces behind the gravestones, peeping at his black veil. It was noticed that he himself hated the sight of the veil and avoided mirrors. This

115 convinced some people that he had committed a terrible crime. The minister seemed to walk in a cloud of sin or sorrow. Love or sympathy could never reach him.

The black veil had one desirable effect. It made him a more effective clergyman. Sinners converted to belief because they felt they

120 had been with him behind the veil, and the dying begged him to come to them. Strangers came from far away to attend his church. He was even asked to preach the election sermon for the governor's administration.[4]

4. **"election sermon for the governor's administration":** Hawthorne is referring to Governor Jonathan Belcher, who governed Massachusetts from 1730–1741.

THE MINISTER'S BLACK VEIL **69**

Here's HOW

VOCABULARY

There's the word *mortal* again, in line 101. It meant "living person" on the previous page. It can't mean that here because Mr. Hooper is talking about a veil. I think here he means a veil "for this lifetime."

Your TURN

SYMBOL

The black veil affects Mr. Hooper's life in many ways. In lines 107–117, circle two ways in which he changes his habits after he starts wearing the veil.

Your TURN

MAKING INFERENCES

Re-read lines 118–123. Why do you think the veil makes Mr. Hooper a better minister?

_____

_____

_____

_____

_____

_____

_____

Here's
HOW

VOCABULARY

Lines 124-125 contain the phrase "lonely and shrouded in suspicions." I think *shrouded* means something like "covered." The dictionary agrees and also says another meaning of *shroud* is a "cloth used to cover a dead person."

Your
TURN

MAKING INFERENCES

In line 130, Hawthorne calls the human heart the "saddest of all prisons." How could the heart be a prison?

_____

_____

_____

Your
TURN

SYMBOL

In lines 142–143, Mr. Hooper claims to see a black veil on every face. What do you think he means? Write your answer on the lines below.

_____

_____

_____

_____

_____

And thus Mr. Hooper spent a long life, lonely and shrouded in
125 suspicions. He was kind and loving, though unloved. People ignored
him when they were healthy and joyous, but they summoned him
when they were dying.

Finally, Mr. Hooper lay dying. Elizabeth came to take care of him,
and church members surrounded him. He still wore the black veil that
130 had kept him in that saddest of all prisons, his own heart.

His mind was confused now and wavered between the past
and the present. But still he would not let the veil be removed. At
last, the attending minister announced that death was near. "Are
you ready," he asked Mr. Hooper, "to lift the veil that shuts in time
135 from eternity?"

"Never," the veiled man cried. With a mighty effort he sat up
and spoke. "Why do you tremble at me alone?" he said. "Tremble
also at each other! Have men avoided me, and women shown no
pity, and children screamed and fled, only for my black veil? What
140 has made this piece of cloth so awful? When all are open and
honest and pure with each other, showing their inmost selves, then
call me a monster. I look around me and, lo, on every face I see a
Black Veil!"

And so he died. They laid him, still veiled, in his coffin and bore
145 him to his grave. Grass has grown for many years on that grave,
and the burial stone is grown over with moss. The minister's face is
dust; but awful still is the thought that it rotted beneath the Black
Veil!

Symbol

A **symbol** is something that has meaning itself but also stands for something more than itself. In Hawthorne's story you have read about the black veil. It is a symbol that separates its wearer from the world. As the story unfolds, the veil takes on different meanings, including sin and sorrow.

You see many symbols every day. Red traffic lights mean "stop." Two fingers forming a *V* means "victory." In the left-hand column below are descriptions of common symbols you probably have seen before. Match them with their meanings in the right-hand column. Draw a line from each symbol to its meaning. One symbol has already been done for you.

Symbol	Meaning
1. an American flag	**a.** surrender
2. scales held up by blindfolded woman	**b.** freedom; welcome to all
3. Statue of Liberty	**c.** patriotism
4. a white flag	**d.** international cooperation; athletic achievement
5. the five Olympic rings	**e.** fairness; justice

The Pit and the Pendulum

Literary Focus: Symbolic Meaning

When you read a story, you may sometimes sense that it has a deeper meaning that goes beyond what happens on the surface level. For example, if a young girl in a story is in a conflict with her parents over a pair of earrings, you might guess that the earrings symbolize something important to her—such as self-expression or independence. A **symbol** is an object, person, animal, or place that functions as itself but also has a deeper meaning.

What does each of these familiar symbols represent?

Reading Skill: Retelling

It is a good idea to stop at key points in a story and **retell** in your own words what has happened so far. This retelling strategy will help you understand and remember the story.

Into the Short Story

Edgar Allan Poe's frightening stories have inspired many of today's mystery and horror writers. In fact, the Mystery Writers of America honors great works in the field with an award named after Poe—the Edgar. Here is his famous horror story of a man sentenced to death and placed in an extraordinary prison cell in Toledo, Spain. Since the story is told from the first-person point of view—by the prisoner himself—you know that he will survive the torture. Or will he?

The Pit and the Pendulum

BASED ON THE SHORT STORY BY
Edgar Allan Poe

Here's HOW

SYMBOLIC MEANING

The black-robed, white-lipped judges (line 2) remind me of the figure of death with his face hidden by a black-hooded robe. The judges are probably symbols of death.

Your TURN

SYMBOLIC MEANING

Stop at line 8. What do you think the dark place deep below the earth symbolizes? Write your answer on the lines below.

_____

_____

_____

Here's HOW

RETELLING

In lines 1–16, the prisoner is sentenced to death. He faints and is carried to a dark cell, deep in the earth. He feels his way around the cold, slimy walls, but when he tries to cross the room, he falls down. He finds himself at the edge of a deep, smelly pit. He realizes his captors plan for him a slow horrible death.

YOU NEED TO KNOW The Spanish Inquisition was a religious court set up by the Catholic Church and the Spanish government in the 1400s. Its role was to accuse and punish anyone who defied church or government authority.

The death sentence was the last thing I heard. After that, I saw the white lips of the black-robed judges move but heard no sound. Then I fainted, and silence and darkness surrounded me.

Tall, silent figures carried me down—down—still down—into a
5 flat, damp place. After a time, I opened my eyes. My worst fears came true; the blackness of eternal night surrounded me. I struggled for breath. Those sentenced to death by the Spanish Inquisition were usually burned at the stake. What will happen to me?

I felt my way around the cell. The stone walls were slimy and cold
10 as I slowly made my way around them. Then, as I tried to cross the moist, slippery floor, my robe tangled in my legs and I fell. I shuddered to find my chin resting on the edge of a deep pit that stank of decay.

I realized my captors had meant for me to fall into this horrible
15 pit. A quick and easy death was not part of their plan! A slow hideous death awaited me!

At last, I slept. When I woke, a dim blue light showed me that the prison was roughly square and far smaller than I had first thought. The walls seemed to me now to be some kind of huge metal plates.
20 These were painted with frightening pictures of fiends and skeletons. The center of the floor fell away into the round pit, which I had just avoided.

I now lay stretched on a low wooden rack. A long strap wound many times around my body, leaving only my head and left arm free
25 enough that I could feed myself from a dish which lay by my side. It seemed my tormentors meant to torture me with thirst—for the meat in the dish was highly seasoned.

The ceiling was thirty feet overhead. I noticed a strange figure painted there, a picture of Time holding what I thought was a huge clock pendulum. But while I gazed straight upward at the pendulum, I realized it was not a painting but an actual pendulum, which swung slowly back and forth.

Perhaps an hour passed before I looked upward again. What I then saw amazed me. The swing of the pendulum and its speed had both increased. But what mainly bothered me was that it was *lower*. I now saw that its weight was a curved steel blade, with a razor-sharp edge. Since I had not fallen into the hell-like pit as they hoped, the torturers had made a new and different death for me: I should be slowly sliced in two as the pendulum inched down. For what seemed like days, the sharp blade lowered itself toward me!

Then a vague hope came into my mind. As the pendulum swung across my body, I saw it would cross over my heart. I now realized that the strap which bound me was *continuous*. The blade's first stroke on any part of the band would cut it so I might unwind myself with my free left hand. I lifted my head enough to see my chest. The strap tied my body tightly in all directions—*except in the path of the destroying blade*. The pendulum would first slice my body and not the strap.

Then another idea of rescue came to me. For many hours the area round the low framework upon which I lay had been swarming with rats. They were wild, bold—their red eyes glaring at me, waiting only for me to lie still before they began to feast upon me. With the remaining bits of the oily food, I rubbed the ties wherever I could reach them. Then, raising my hand from the floor, I lay perfectly still. Perhaps now the rats could be tempted to gnaw me loose.

Eventually, one or two of the boldest rats leaped upon the framework and sniffed the belt. Behind them many more swarmed upon me in heaps and gnawed on the greasy loops. I felt the ties loosen. I knew that it must be already cut in several places. With a more than human courage I lay *still*.

At last, I felt that I was free. The belt hung in ribbons from my body. But the pendulum already pressed upon me. It had slit the fibers of the robe, but my moment of escape had arrived. With a cautious, slow, steady movement, I slid from the ties and beyond the reach of the blade. For the moment, at least, *I was free.*

Your
TURN

RETELLING

Stop at line 40, and retell what has happened in lines 23–40.

_____

_____

_____

_____

_____

_____

_____

_____

Here's
HOW

SYMBOLIC MEANING

Father Time with his scythe is a well-known symbol of death. A clock pendulum is a symbol of time. I'd guess that their symbolic meaning is that time is running out for the poor prisoner.

Your
TURN

SYMBOLIC MEANING

What do you think the swarming rats symbolize to the prisoner?

_____

_____

_____

65   *Free!*—yet still in the grasp of the Inquisition! I had barely moved
from my wooden bed of horror when the motion of the hellish blade
stopped, and I saw it pulled up through the ceiling. I had only
exchanged one form of agony for another, maybe worse than death.
But now something else which I could not understand had happened
70 in the dungeon. For many minutes I sat thinking about it.

    Then the nature of the chamber's change came to me all at once. The
colored figures on the walls had now taken on an intense gleam. Demon
eyes, wildly alive, glared at me from every side and shone like fire.

    As I breathed, I smelled the odor of heated iron! The walls and
75 ceiling began to glow! There could be no doubt what my tormentors
meant to do—they were firing the iron walls to roast me to death!

    I shrank away from the glowing metal—to the center of the cell.
With the thought of the fiery death ahead, the idea of the well's
coolness came over me. I rushed to its deadly edge, straining to see
80 below. The glare from the burning ceiling lit its deepest parts. At last
I understood what I saw—the bones and rotten flesh, the rats still
gnawing on them—oh! any horror but this! With a shriek, I rushed
from the edge and buried my face in my hands—weeping bitterly.

    The heat rapidly increased, and once again I looked up. There had
85 been a second change in the cell—a change in its *shape*. The
Inquisitors' revenge had sped up, and there was to be no more
playing games. The room had been square, but now the cell shifted
into a diamond shape. Now I was so desperate for relief that I could
have hugged the red walls to my breast, giving myself up to eternal
90 peace. "Death," I said, "any death except that of the pit!" Fool! Could
I not see that the burning iron was meant to urge me *into the pit*?

    I shrank back—but the closing walls pressed me onward. Finally,
for my scorched and writhing body, there was no longer an inch on
the floor to stand. I struggled no more, but my agony was released in
95 one loud, long, and final scream of despair. I felt that I tottered upon
the edge—I closed my eyes—

    There was a noise of human voices, a loud blast as of many
trumpets! There was a harsh grating as of a thousand thunders! The
fiery walls rushed back! An outstretched arm caught my own as I fell,
100 fainting. The French army had entered Toledo. The Inquisition was in
the hands of its enemies.

Symbolic Meaning

To figure out the **symbolic meaning** of a story, you first think about what all the individual symbols mean. Then you combine all those meanings to come up with the symbolic meaning of the story as a whole. To determine the symbolic meaning of "The Pit and the Pendulum," fill in the meanings of the symbols listed below. Then, decide what the symbolic meaning of the whole story is. One has been done for you.

Symbol	Meaning
1. Cell and pit, deep below the earth	
2. Father Time and the pendulum	
3. Strap wrapped around the prisoner	
4. Rats	Death, decay, torture, horror
5. Hot walls moving toward the prisoner	

Symbolic meaning of the story:_____

_____

The Raven

Literary Focus: Sound Effects

You've heard cartoon sound effects: *Boing! Sproing!* Those noises help you feel and hear whatever's happening.

Sound effects in poetry do the same thing. They emphasize certain key ideas, feelings, and images. Two kinds of sound effects in poetry are onomatopoeia and alliteration. **Onomatopoeia** (on uh mat uh PEE uh) is using words that imitate sounds, like *bang!* **Alliteration** (uh LIHT uh RAY shun) is repeating consonant sounds in words that are close together, like *P*eter *P*iper or *k*ing *c*obra.

In "The Raven" these sound effects stress eerie words and ideas. They help create the poem's mood of horror.

Reading Skill: Interpreting a Poem

Interpreting a poem is explaining what it means. To interpret a poem, notice something; ask yourself what it means; and then come up with a reasonable answer to your question.

Ask: *What does it mean?*

Notice it:
Here's something . . .

Answer your question:
I think it means_____.

Into the Poem

"The Raven" is one of the world's most famous poems. But Edgar Allan Poe, its author, received only about ten dollars for its publication. One reason for the poem's popularity is its sound effects. Its lively rhythms and clever rhymes make the poem fun to hear and to read aloud. The poem's message, though, is far from happy.

Edgar Allan Poe

The Raven

Here's
HOW

SOUND EFFECTS

I noticed, in lines 2 and 3, that *quaint* and *curious* and *nodded, nearly,* and *napping* really stand out when I read the poem aloud. That must be because they're examples of alliteration. Those repeated first consonants (*k* and *n*) are like part of a tongue twister like *Sally sifts seashells by the seashore*.

Here's
HOW

SOUND EFFECTS

I noticed that, when I said *rustling* (line 13), my voice made a whispery *s* sound—like the sound of curtains blowing in the breeze. *Rustling* imitates the sound it names, so it's an example of onomatopoeia.

Edgar Allan Poe's "The Raven" is a narrative poem. It tells the story of a man who is sad about the death of someone he has loved deeply. As you read, try to imagine the eerie scene and to feel the mood of horror the poem creates.

Once upon a midnight dreary,[1] while I pondered, weak and weary,
Over many a quaint and curious volume of forgotten lore[2]—
While I nodded, nearly napping, suddenly there came a tapping,
As of someone gently rapping, rapping at my chamber door—
5 " 'Tis some visitor," I muttered, "tapping at my chamber door—
Only this and nothing more."

Ah, distinctly I remember it was in the bleak December;
And each separate dying ember[3] wrought its ghost upon the floor.
Eagerly I wished the morrow;—vainly I had sought to borrow
10 From my books surcease[4] of sorrow—sorrow for the lost Lenore—
For the rare and radiant maiden whom the angels name Lenore—
Nameless *here* for evermore.

IN OTHER WORDS   On a gloomy night, the poem's speaker sits studying old books. Just as he is about to fall asleep, he hears a tapping. He tells himself it is just a visitor at the door.

It is during a gloomy December night. He is trying to forget his sadness over the death of Lenore, but studying hasn't helped.

And the silken, sad, uncertain rustling of each purple curtain
Thrilled me—filled me with fantastic terrors never felt before;
15 So that now, to still the beating of my heart, I stood repeating
" 'Tis some visitor entreating entrance at my chamber door—
Some late visitor entreating entrance at my chamber door;—
This it is and nothing more."

---

1. **dreary** (DRIHR ee): gloomy, sorrowful.
2. **lore** (lohr): knowledge or stories.
3. **ember** (EHM buhr): piece of coal or wood glowing in a fire's ashes.
4. **surcease** (sur SEES): an end.

Presently my soul grew stronger; hesitating then no longer,
20 "Sir," said I, "or Madam, truly your forgiveness I implore;[5]
But the fact is I was napping, and so gently you came rapping,
And so faintly you came tapping, tapping at my chamber door,
That I scarce was sure I heard you"—here I opened wide the door;—
      Darkness there and nothing more.

IN OTHER WORDS The rustling of the curtains fills the speaker with terror. His heart races as he tells himself it is just a late visitor.

Soon, he feels braver. He asks the visitor to forgive him for not answering the door. He says that he'd been napping and the tapping had been too quiet for him to hear. He opens the door, but no one is there.

Deep into that darkness peering, long I stood there wondering,
25   fearing,
Doubting, dreaming dreams no mortal[6] ever dared to dream before;
But the silence was unbroken, and the stillness gave no token,
And the only word there spoken was the whispered word, "Lenore?"
This I whispered, and an echo murmured back the word, "Lenore!"
30   Merely this and nothing more.

Back into the chamber turning, all my soul within me burning,
Soon again I heard a tapping somewhat louder than before.
"Surely," said I, "surely that is something at my window lattice;[7]
Let me see, then, what thereat is, and this mystery explore—
35 Let my heart be still a moment and this mystery explore;—
      'Tis the wind and nothing more!"

---

5. **implore** (ihm PLOHR): beg.
6. **mortal** (MAWR tuhl): human being.
7. **lattice** (LAT ihs): criss-crossing wooden strips with open spaces between them.

Here's HOW

INTERPRETING A POEM

In lines 25–26, the guy's just staring off into darkness. Is he wondering when a visitor will get there? Is he thinking about Lenore? Maybe he's imagining that Lenore's going to visit. Maybe he wishes she'd come back from the dead. That might explain why he whispers her name in line 29. It could also explain why he's "fearing" and "doubting." He might want to see Lenore, but he'd be afraid if she were a ghost. And, since she's dead, he'd doubt that she was there.

Your TURN

SOUND EFFECTS

Circle words in line 29 that are examples of onomatopoeia.

Here's HOW

VOCABULARY

The word *thereat* (line 34) looks like it might be a word we don't use anymore. It sounds like "there at," but I wasn't sure whether "there at" fit the sentence. I looked *thereat* up in a dictionary. It means "at that place." My guess was pretty close.

Your
TURN

SOUND EFFECTS

In line 43, Poe uses alliteration to stress where the raven lands. Circle the words with the same consonant sounds in that line.

Here's
HOW

INTERPRETING A POEM

It's strange that the raven lands on a statue of the Greek goddess of wisdom. What does that mean? Does the bird like statues? Does it like Greek goddesses? I'll bet it's important that it's the goddess of wisdom. I'll bet the bird's going to teach the guy something. He'd better listen to whatever that raven says.

Here's
HOW

VOCABULARY

I didn't recognize the word *shorn* in the line that begins "'Though thy crest'" (line 45). Then I remembered that some verbs in English form their tenses irregularly, like *bear–born* or *tear–torn*. I guessed that *shorn* might be a form of *shear*. When I looked it up, I was right! *Shorn* is the past participle of *shear*.

IN OTHER WORDS   The speaker stares into the darkness. He whispers, "Lenore?" An echo comes back, "Lenore!"

He steps back, and the tapping starts again, louder than before. He tells himself that something is at the window. His heart races. He tries to calm down so that he can find out what is there. He thinks that it is only the wind.

Open here I flung the shutter, when, with many a flirt and flutter,
In there stepped a stately Raven of the saintly days of yore;[8]
Not the least obeisance[9] made he; not a minute stopped or stayed he;
40   But, with mien[10] of lord or lady, perched above my chamber door—
Perched upon a bust of Pallas[11] just above my chamber door—
      Perched, and sat, and nothing more.

Then this ebony bird beguiling[12] my sad fancy into smiling,
By the grave and stern decorum of the countenance[13] it wore,
"Though thy crest be shorn and shaven, thou," I said, "art sure no
45   craven,[14]
Ghastly grim and ancient Raven wandering from the Nightly shore—
Tell me what thy lordly name is on the Night's Plutonian shore!"[15]
      Quoth the Raven "Nevermore."

IN OTHER WORDS   The speaker throws the shutter open. A raven steps in, then flies up and perches on a sculpture of the Greek goddess Athena.

The speaker smiles at the bird's stern and serious look. He tells the bird that although its head feathers have been cut, it is not a coward. He asks its name. It answers, "Nevermore."

---

8. **Raven . . . of yore:** "Of yore" is an old way of saying "long ago." Poe refers to a Bible story in which the hungry prophet Elijah is fed by ravens. (1 Kings 17:1–6)
9. **obeisance** (oh BAY suns): gesture of respect or subservience.
10. **mien** (meen): appearance.
11. **Pallas:** Pallas Athena, in Greek mythology, the goddess of wisdom.
12. **beguiling** (bih GY lihng): charming.
13. **decorum of the countenance:** formality of expression.
14. **craven** (KRAY vuhn): coward.
15. **Plutonian shore:** In Greek mythology, Pluto is the god of the underworld, a land of darkness separated from the land of the living by the river Styx.

Much I marveled this ungainly[16] fowl to hear discourse[17] so plainly,

50 Though its answer little meaning—little relevancy bore;

For we cannot help agreeing that no living human being

Ever yet was blessed with seeing bird above his chamber door—

Bird or beast upon the sculptured bust above his chamber door,

     With such name as "Nevermore."

55 But the Raven, sitting lonely on the placid[18] bust, spoke only

That one word, as if his soul in that one word he did outpour.

Nothing farther then he uttered—not a feather then he fluttered—

Till I scarcely more than muttered "Other friends have flown before—

On the morrow *he* will leave me, as my Hopes have flown before."

60   Then the bird said "Nevermore."

IN OTHER WORDS The speaker doesn't understand the bird's answer. He decides that this has never happened before.

The bird says nothing else until the speaker says that the bird will leave in the morning. He says he's had other friends and hopes that flew away. The bird answers, "Nevermore."

Startled at the stillness broken by reply so aptly[19] spoken,

"Doubtless," said I, "what it utters is its only stock and store

Caught from some unhappy master whom unmerciful Disaster

Followed fast and followed faster till his songs one burden bore—

65 Till the dirges[20] of his Hope that melancholy burden bore

     Of 'Never—nevermore.' "

But the Raven still beguiling my sad fancy[21] into smiling,

Straight I wheeled a cushioned seat in front of bird, and bust and door;

Then, upon the velvet sinking, I betook myself to linking

70 Fancy unto fancy, thinking what this ominous[22] bird of yore—

---

16. ungainly: clumsy.
17. discourse: speak.
18. placid (PLAS ihd): quiet and peaceful.
19. aptly: appropriately.
20. dirges (DURJ ihz): songs sung at funerals.
21. fancy: imagination.
22. ominous (OM uh nuhs): threatening.

Your
TURN

SOUND EFFECTS

In line 58, Poe uses onomatopoeia to stress how the speaker sounds. Circle a word that is an example of onomatopoeia in line 58.

Your
TURN

INTERPRETING A POEM

In lines 58–59, the speaker says, "Other friends have flown before—On the morrow *he* will leave me, as my Hopes have flown before." What do you think the speaker means?

_____

_____

_____

_____

_____

_____

_____

_____

_____

_____

_____

Your
TURN

Your
TURN

What this grim, ungainly, ghastly, gaunt, and ominous bird of yore
   Meant in croaking "Nevermore."

IN OTHER WORDS The speaker is surprised at the appropriateness of the bird's answer, but he decides it had been trained to talk by an unhappy master.

 Amused, he smiles, rolls a seat in front of the door, and looks up at the bird. Then he begins to imagine what the raven means in saying, "Nevermore."

This I sat engaged in guessing, but no syllable expressing
To the fowl whose fiery eyes now burned into my bosom's core;
75 This and more I sat divining,[23] with my head at ease reclining
On the cushion's velvet lining that the lamplight gloated o'er,
But whose velvet-violet lining with the lamplight gloating o'er,
   She shall press, ah, nevermore!

Then, methought, the air grew denser, perfumed from an unseen
   censer[24]
80 Swung by seraphim[25] whose footfalls tinkled on the tufted floor.
"Wretch," I cried, "thy God hath lent thee—by these angels he hath
   sent thee
Respite—respite and nepenthe[26] from thy memories of Lenore;
Quaff, oh quaff[27] this kind nepenthe and forget this lost Lenore!"
   Quoth the Raven "Nevermore."

IN OTHER WORDS The speaker sits thinking. He feels as though the raven's eyes burn into his heart. He leans his head back against the velvet cushion. Then he realizes that Lenore will never rest her head against that same cushion again.

---

23. **divining:** inferring or discovering.
24. **censer** (SEHN suhr): container used to burn incense.
25. **seraphim** (SAYR uh fim): supposedly the highest of the nine ranks of angels; often pictured as having three sets of wings.
26. **nepenthe** (nee PEN thee): a sleeping potion that people once believed would relieve pain and sorrow. Eventually it came to stand for anything that brought such relief.
27. **quaff** (kwahf): take deep drinks.

He imagines that the air grew thick with the smell of incense burned by an invisible angel. Suddenly, he yells that God and the angels have sent the raven to help him get over Lenore. He asks whether anything could help him forget her. The raven answers, "Nevermore."

85 "Prophet!" said I, "thing of evil!—prophet still, if bird or devil!—
Whether Tempter sent, or whether tempest tossed thee here
    ashore,
Desolate yet all undaunted, on this desert land enchanted—
On this home by Horror haunted—tell me truly, I implore—
Is there—*is* there balm in Gilead?[28]—tell me—tell me, I implore!"
90   Quoth the Raven "Nevermore."

"Prophet!" said I, "thing of evil!—prophet still, if bird or devil!
By that Heaven that bends above us—by that God we both adore—
Tell this soul with sorrow laden if, within the distant Aidenn,[29]
It shall clasp a sainted maiden whom the angels name Lenore—
95 Clasp a rare and radiant maiden whom the angels name Lenore."
       Quoth the Raven "Nevermore."

"Be that word our sign of parting, bird or fiend!" I shrieked,
    upstarting—
"Get thee back into the tempest and the Night's Plutonian shore!
Leave no black plume[30] as a token of that lie thy soul hath spoken!
100 Leave my loneliness unbroken!—quit the bust above my door!
Take thy beak from out my heart, and take thy form from off my
    door!"
       Quoth the Raven "Nevermore."

INTERPRETING A POEM

Re-read lines 93–99. After the raven says "Nevermore" in line 96, the speaker gets terribly angry. Why do you think he gets so angry?

_____

_____

_____

_____

VOCABULARY

The old word *quoth* appears five times in this poem (lines 48, 84, 90, 96, and 102). What modern word does *quoth* remind you of? How would you define *quoth*?

_____

_____

_____

_____

---

28. *is . . . Gilead?* "Is there any relief from my sorrow?" Poe restates a line from the Bible's Jeremiah 8:22: "Is there no balm in Gilead?" Gilead was a place known for its healing herbs, such as balm. Balm has come to mean "any healing ointment."
29. **Aidenn:** Arabic for "Eden" or "Heaven."
30. **plume** (ploom): feather.

INTERPRETING A POEM

What do you think this last stanza (lines 103–108) means?

_____

_____

_____

_____

_____

_____

_____

_____

IN OTHER WORDS   Angered by the bird's reply, the speaker says that he can't tell whether the raven is a prophet of good or of evil. He asks if he'll ever have relief from his sorrow. The raven says, "Nevermore."

Then he asks the bird whether he'll be able to hug Lenore in heaven one day. The raven answers, "Nevermore."

The speaker becomes angrier. He jumps up and screams at the bird. He tells it to go back to the underworld and to leave him alone with his own loneliness. The raven replies, "Nevermore."

And the Raven, never flitting, still is sitting, *still* is sitting
On the pallid bust of Pallas just above my chamber door;
105 And his eyes have all the seeming of a demon's that is dreaming,
And the lamplight o'er him streaming throws his shadow on the floor;
And my soul from out that shadow that lies floating on the floor
     Shall be lifted—nevermore!

IN OTHER WORDS   The speaker says that the demon raven has never flown away. It is still staring down at him from the statue. The speaker says his spirits will never be lifted.

Sound Effects

Poets use sound effects to make their poems musical and to emphasize certain key ideas, feelings, and images.

- **Alliteration** is the repetition of consonant sounds in words that are close together.
- **Onomatopoeia** is the use of words that imitate the sounds they describe.

A. In each of the following lines from "The Raven," draw a circle around the words that are examples of **alliteration**. One example has been provided for you. Notice that the repeating consonant sound doesn't always come at the beginning of a word. Also, don't forget that different letters sometimes have the same sound.

1. And the silken, sad, uncertain rustling of each purple curtain

2. Thrilled me—filled me with fantastic terrors never felt before;

3. Doubting, dreaming dreams no mortal ever dared to dream before;

4. Bird or beast upon the sculptured bust above his chamber door,

5. Whether Tempter sent, or whether tempest tossed thee here ashore,

B. On the lines below, write three sentences of your own, using **onomatopoeia.** Then, underline each example of onomatopoeia in your sentences. If you want, you may use three of the following onomatopoeic words in your sentences: *buzz, slap, splash, hiss, growl.*

1. _____

_____

2. _____

_____

3. _____

_____

American Masters:
Whitman and Dickinson
Based on the Student Edition text by John Malcolm Brinnin

The two greatest American poets of the nineteenth century had little in common. Only a nation as diverse as the United States could have produced them both.

5 Both Walt Whitman and Emily Dickinson were close observers of people and of daily life. But they viewed their art and their roles as poets very differently. Whitman was active and outgoing. He saw himself as a spokesperson, a prophet[1] of democracy. "I hear America singing," he said, and he boldly added his own voice to the chorus. Dickinson, though, was private and shy. Looking through the curtains 10 of her house, she saw a nature full of symbols and metaphors. She recorded these images with no hope of an audience. Whitman expected his message to be carried into the future, but Dickinson expected her poetry to remain unknown.

Two Seams in the Fabric

15 As a young man, Whitman drifted from place to place and job to job. He did not truly "find himself" until his mid-thirties, when he used his own money to publish a collection of poetry called *Leaves of Grass* (1855). The book made Whitman famous. Dickinson's poetry, on the other hand, was discovered and published only after her death.

20 Whitman and Dickinson represent two different seams in the fabric of American poetry. One seam is rambling and uneven; the other is careful and tight. Whitman unleashed his passions and his thoughts in a flood of words. Aiming to capture the "big picture," he filled his poems with lists of everything in sight. Whitman's **free verse**

---

1. **prophet** (PRAHF iht): one who publicly tells what will happen in the future.

poems do not have set rhymes or rhythms. Instead, they follow long, sweeping **cadences,** like the rise and fall of an impassioned speech.

Unlike Whitman, Dickinson wrote verse that was focused and exact. She chose each word with great care, striving to communicate shades of meaning and feeling. Her stanzas[2] follow a set pattern of rhyme and meter,[3] much like the musical patterns she found in her hymnbook.

Models for Future Poets

Both Whitman and Dickinson have served as models for the poets who came after them. Like Whitman, some modern writers see poetry as public speech or are drawn to the cadences of free verse. Others, like Dickinson, see poetry as private, carefully crafted gems. Together these different styles and approaches—and all those in between— make up the American poetic tradition.

Here's HOW

VOCABULARY

The word *cadences* in line 26 has me stumped. I'd better look it up. The dictionary says that cadences are the ups and downs of the voice. So in poetry they are part of the rhythm.

2. **stanzas** (STAN zuhz): lines of a poem grouped together, separated from other lines by spaces.
3. **meter:** pattern of stressed and unstressed syllables in poetry.

From Song of Myself, Numbers 10, 33, and 52

Literary Focus: Free Verse

Many of the poems you've read probably use a regular rhyme scheme and meter. (Roses are red. / Violets are blue. / I feel hungry. / How about you?) But some poems don't use a regular rhyme and meter. These poems are written in **free verse.** Although they do not follow a regular rhyme or meter, free verse poems use other poetic elements, such as

- **alliteration**—repetition of similar consonant sounds
- **assonance**—repetition of similar vowel sounds
- **imagery**—language that appeals to the senses
- **onomatopoeia**—use of words whose sounds echo their meaning
- **parallel structure**—repetition of phrases or sentences that have the same grammatical structure
- **cadence**—musical rise and fall of the voice

Look for these poetic elements as you read Whitman's poems.

Reading Skill: Making Inferences

Making inferences is a lot like being a detective. You use your own experiences and knowledge as well as evidence from the text to make inferences, or educated guesses, about what is happening and why.

Into the Poem

Walt Whitman's *Song of Myself* is a long exploration of feelings about what it means to be American. The poem lovingly examines the lives and activities of all kinds of people from across the nation.

　　As you read the following selections from the poem, watch closely for Whitman's insights into the emotions and experiences of the people he describes.

Walt Whitman

FROM *Song of Myself*

FREE VERSE

In lines 1–5, I see that the poem does not rhyme or have a regular meter. What other elements of poetry does it have? Ah, I see that lines 2, 4, and 5 have parallel structure—they all start with the same part of speech.

MAKING INFERENCES

I didn't understand why someone would lean over the front of the ship or shout from its deck (line 7). Then I asked myself, "What would make me act that way?" My answer is this: Being really happy to see land again. I guess the sailor's been at sea for a long, long time. Now he's happy to be close to shore again.

YOU NEED TO KNOW   In *Song of Myself,* the poet Walt Whitman shares in the thoughts and feelings of a variety of American characters, from slaves to military generals.

Whitman felt that looking into the lives of other Americans could connect citizens to each other in a powerful way. He wanted Americans to see their nation as a single, wonderful whole.

10

Alone far in the wilds and mountains I hunt,
Wandering amazed at my own lightness and glee,
In the late afternoon choosing a safe spot to pass the night,
Kindling[1] a fire and broiling the fresh-kill'd game,[2]
Falling asleep on the gather'd leaves with my dog and gun by my
5   side.

The Yankee clipper is under her sky-sails,[3] she cuts the sparkle
    and scud,[4]
My eyes settle the land, I bend at her prow[5] or shout joyously from
    the deck.

The boatmen and clam-diggers arose early and stopt for me,
I tuck'd my trowser-ends in my boots and went and had a good
    time;
10 You should have been with us that day round the chowder-kettle.

IN OTHER WORDS   First, the speaker adopts the voice of a hunter. Although he hunts alone, he is amazed at how happy he is. He enjoys his simple life in the wilderness.

Next, the speaker adopts the voice of a seaman. He shouts joyfully when he sees land. Later, he and other sailors have an excellent time together and at dinner.

---

1. **kindling:** setting a fire.
2. **game:** wild animals hunted for food or sport.
3. **sky-sails:** small sails atop a ship's mast.
4. **scud:** windblown sea spray or foam.
5. **her prow:** the pointed front of the ship.

I saw the marriage of the trapper in the open air in the far west, the bride was a red girl,

Her father and his friends sat near cross-legged and dumbly smoking, they had moccasins[6] to their feet and large thick blankets hanging from their shoulders,

On a bank lounged the trapper, he was drest mostly in skins, his luxuriant beard and curls protected his neck, he held his bride by the hand,

She had long eyelashes, her head was bare, her coarse straight locks[7] descended upon her voluptuous limbs and reach'd to her feet.

15 The runaway slave came to my house and stopt outside,

I heard his motions crackling the twigs of the woodpile,

Through the swung half-door of the kitchen I saw him limpsy[8] and weak,

And went where he sat on a log and led him in and assured him,

And brought water and fill'd a tub for his sweated body and bruis'd feet,

And gave him a room that enter'd from my own, and gave him

20 some coarse clean clothes,

And remember perfectly well his revolving eyes and his awkwardness,

And remember putting plasters[9] on the galls[10] of his neck and ankles;

He stayed with me a week before he was recuperated[11] and pass'd north,

I had him sit next me at table, my fire-lock[12] lean'd in the corner.

---

6. **moccasins** (MOK uh suhnz): soft shoes made of deer leather.
7. **locks:** hair.
8. **limpsy:** limp; exhausted.
9. **plasters:** medical ointment spread on a cloth, used to relieve pain.
10. **galls:** sores.
11. **recuperated** (rih KYOO puh rayt uhd): restored to health.
12. **fire-lock:** gun, such as a flintlock.

Here's HOW

MAKING INFERENCES

Why does the speaker say that the bride was "red" in line 11? I remember some things we learned in social studies class. People used to say Native Americans had red skin. Also, many of the first Europeans to head west were fur trappers. I'll bet that's what's happening. A fur trapper is marrying a Native American girl he met in the western mountains.

Your TURN

MAKING INFERENCES

Underline the clues in lines 15–24 that tell you that the runaway slave's journey north has been difficult and dangerous.

Your TURN

FREE VERSE

A poetic element often used in free verse is alliteration—the repetition of consonant sounds in nearby words. What sound is most often repeated in lines 21–23? Write it below, and then circle all the words that begin with that sound:

_____

Your
TURN

IN OTHER WORDS First, the speaker tells of watching the outdoor wedding of a fur trapper and a Native American girl. He describes the bride's father, the wedding guests, and the groom and bride.

Next, he talks about finding an escaped slave outside his home. He brings the runaway slave inside, allows him to wash, and gives him a room in which to stay. He helps the runaway slave recover from his wounds, gives him clean clothes, and feeds him. After a week, the man continues his journey north.

from 33

I understand the large hearts of heroes,
The courage of present times and all times,
How the skipper saw the crowded and rudderless[1] wreck of the
    steam-ship, and Death chasing it up and down the storm,
How he knuckled tight and gave not back an inch, and was
    faithful of days and faithful of nights,
And chalk'd in large letters on a board, _Be of good cheer, we will_
5   _not desert you;_
How he follow'd with them and tack'd[2] with them three days and
    would not give it up,
How he saved the drifting company at last,
How the lank[3] loose-gown'd women look'd when boated from the
    side of their prepared graves,
How the silent old-faced infants and the lifted sick, and the sharp-
    lipp'd unshaved men;
10 All this I swallow, it tastes good, I like it well, it becomes mine,
I am the man, I suffer'd, I was there.[4]

---

1. **rudderless:** missing the steering portion of the ship.
2. **tack'd:** sailed against the wind in a zigzag course.
3. **lank:** slender.
4. **I understand . . . I was there:** A copy of a newspaper story about a similar incident was found among Whitman's papers after his death. A violent storm hit a ship, washing many passengers overboard. The captain of another ship helped rescue the survivors.

IN OTHER WORDS The speaker says he understands heroism. He tells the story of a wrecked ship. Despite a dangerous storm, another ship followed it for three days. The captain of the rescuing ship held up a sign telling people aboard the wreck that he would stay with them. The speaker knows what the passengers and crew experienced.

The disdain[5] and calmness of martyrs,[6]
The mother of old, condemn'd for a witch, burnt with dry wood,
    her children gazing on,
The hounded slave that flags[7] in the race, leans by the fence,
    blowing, cover'd with sweat,
The twinges that sting like needles his legs and neck, the

15   murderous buckshot[8] and the bullets,
All these I feel or am.
I am the hounded slave, I wince at the bite of the dogs,
Hell and despair are upon me, crack and again crack the
    marksmen,
I clutch the rails of the fence, my gore dribs,[9] thinn'd with the
    ooze of my skin,

20 I fall on the weeds and stones,
The riders spur their unwilling horses, haul close,
Taunt my dizzy ears and beat me violently over the head with
    whip-stocks.

Agonies are one of my changes of garments,
I do not ask the wounded person how he feels, I myself become
    the wounded person,

25 My hurts turn livid[10] upon me as I lean on a cane and observe.

---

5. **disdain** (dihs TAYN): scorn.
6. **martyrs** (MAHR tuhrz): people put to death for their beliefs.
7. **flags**: grows weak and tired.
8. **buckshot** (BUHK shot): lead shot used to shoot large animals.
9. **gore dribs**: dribbles of thick blood.
10. **livid** (LIHV ihd): pale or black and blue, the color of a bruise.

Your TURN

FREE VERSE

Underline the clues in line 13 that tell you how and why the "mother of old" died.

Your TURN

FREE VERSE

Assonance—repetition of similar vowel sounds in nearby words—is another element of poetry often found in free verse. Circle the examples of assonance in line 16.

Your TURN

FREE VERSE

Parallel structure is a common element of Whitman's poetry. Underline the repeated grammatical structures in lines 17, 19, and 20.

Here's
HOW

FREE VERSE

One of the poetic elements I learned about is imagery. Lines 26–30 have images that appeal to three different senses. I see the wounded fireman buried under fallen walls. I feel the heat and smoke. I hear the shouts and the clicks of the shovels. And I feel friends lifting gently.

Your
TURN

MAKING INFERENCES

In this poem, Whitman frequently repeats the phrase "I am" (lines 11, 17, 26, 37, 38) when he describes very different people. What idea do you think he is emphasizing with this repetition?

_____

_____

_____

_____

Here's
HOW

FREE VERSE

I can find two elements of poetry in lines 39–41. There is parallel structure in the repetition of "Again," and there is alliteration in the *r* sounds in "roll," "drummers," "mortars," and "responsive." Both these elements help create the sense of the guns firing and the drums banging.

I am the mash'd fireman with breast-bone broken,

Tumbling walls buried me in their debris,[11]

Heat and smoke I inspired,[12] I heard the yelling shouts of my
    comrades,

I heard the distant click of their picks and shovels,

30   They have clear'd the beams away, they tenderly lift me forth.

I lie in the night air in my red shirt, the pervading hush is for my
    sake,

Painless after all I lie exhausted but not so unhappy,

White and beautiful are the faces around me, the heads are
    bared of their fire-caps,

The kneeling crowd fades with the light of the torches.

35   Distant and dead resuscitate,[13]

They show as the dial or move as the hands of me, I am the
    clock myself.

I am an old artillerist,[14] I tell of my fort's bombardment,[15]

I am there again.

Again the long roll of the drummers,

40   Again the attacking cannon, mortars,[16]

Again to my listening ears the cannon responsive.

I take part, I see and hear the whole,

The cries, curses, roar, the plaudits[17] for well-aim'd shots,

The ambulanza slowly passing trailing its red drip,

Workmen searching after damages, making indispensable

45   repairs,

The fall of grenades through the rent roof, the fan-shaped
    explosion,

The whizz of limbs, heads, stone, wood, iron, high in the air.

---

11. **debris** (duh BREE): scattered pieces.
12. **inspired:** breathed.
13. **resuscitate** (rih SUHS uh tayt): revive.
14. **artillerist** (ahrt IHL uhr ihst): soldier with the artillery, gunner.
15. **bombardment** (bom BAHRD muhnt): bombing with artillery shells.
16. **mortars** (MAWR tuhrz): short cannons.
17. **plaudits** (PLAW dihts): expressions of support.

Again gurgles the mouth of my dying general, he furiously waves
    with his hand,
He gasps through the clot *Mind not me—mind—the
    entrenchments.*[18]

IN OTHER WORDS   The speaker describes the courage of martyrs, people who have suffered and died for a cause. He tells of a woman burned as a witch. Then he describes the agonies of a runaway slave who has been shot and beaten to death. He talks of a fireman who has been killed by a falling wall, and he describes his funeral. Finally, he tells the story of a dying general. As one of the general's men tries to help him, the general scolds the soldier, telling him to worry about the battle, instead.

52

The spotted hawk swoops by and accuses me, he complains of my
    gab and my loitering.[1]

I too am not a bit tamed, I too am untranslatable,
I sound my barbaric yawp over the roofs of the world.

The last scud[2] of day holds back for me,
It flings my likeness after the rest and true as any on the
5   shadow'd wilds,
It coaxes me to the vapor and the dusk.

I depart as air, I shake my white locks at the runaway sun,
I effuse[3] my flesh in eddies,[4] and drift it in lacy jags.[5]

I bequeath[6] myself to the dirt to grow from the grass I love,
10 If you want me again look for me under your boot-soles.

---

  18. entrenchments (ehn TRENCH muhntz): defensive position within trenches.
   1. loitering (LOY tuhr ihng): lazy or frivolous lingering.
   2. scud: windblown sea spray or foam.
   3. effuse (ih FYOOZ): pour out.
   4. eddies: small whirlpools.
   5. jags: uneven tears, as in cloth.
   6. bequeath (bih KWEETH): entrust, leave.

FREE VERSE

Onomatopoeia is the use of words whose sounds echo their meaning. Circle the examples of onomatopoeia in the two lines at the top of the page.

VOCABULARY

Line 3 confused me at first. Then I realized that *sound* is being used as an action word. Here *sound* means "to make a noise." Then I thought about hawks' loud, screeching sounds. I'll bet he's saying his poetry makes loud, screeching noises, just as a hawk does.

MAKING INFERENCES

In lines 9 and 10, the speaker says that he's leaving himself to the dirt and grass. Then he says that we'll have to look for him under our own feet. What do you think he means?

_____
_____
_____
_____
_____
_____
_____

FREE VERSE

How many consonant sounds repeat in lines 13–16? Write the sounds on the lines below. Then, circle all the words in those lines that show alliteration.

_____

_____

_____

_____

You will hardly know who I am or what I mean,
But I shall be good health to you nevertheless,
And filter and fiber your blood.

Failing to fetch me at first keep encouraged,
15 Missing me one place search another,
I stop somewhere waiting for you.

IN OTHER WORDS The speaker says that a hawk objects to his meaningless talk and laziness. Then he points out his similarities to the hawk. He is wild, hard to understand, and shouts out to the world. He says that he is like the clouds at sunset and like the soil under our feet, hardly noticed but good for us all. He says that we may not catch him at first, but we should keep looking for him. Finally, he says that he is out there somewhere, waiting for us to meet him.

Free Verse

Free verse does not follow a regular meter or rhyme scheme, but that does not mean that anything goes. Free-verse poems contain many other elements of poetry.

In the chart below, elements of poetry are listed in the left-hand column. Quotations from "Song of Myself" are listed in the right-hand column. Draw connecting lines showing which element of poetry each quotation is an example of. Some quotes contain more than one element. Choose the one you think the quote most strongly represents. One has been done for you.

Element of Poetry	Quotation from "Song of Myself"
1. **alliteration**—repetition of similar consonant sounds	a. "The twinges that sting like needles his legs and neck"
2. **assonance**—repetition of similar vowel sounds	b. "The Yankee clipper is under her sky-sails, she cuts the sparkle and scud"
3. **imagery**—language that appeals to the senses	c. "I am an old artillerist, I tell of my fort's bombardment,/I am there again."
4. **onomatopoeia**—use of words whose sounds echo their meaning	d. "I effuse my flesh in eddies"
5. **parallel structure**—repetitions of phrases or sentences that have the same grammatical structure	e. "Hell and despair are upon me, crack and again crack the marksmen"

The Soul selects her own Society; Because I could not stop for Death

Literary Focus: Slant Rhyme and Irony

When you think of rhyme, you probably think of **exact rhyme,** in which the accented syllables and all following syllables of two or more words share identical sounds—*free / bee; mixture / fixture.* Emily Dickinson and many modern poets often use **slant rhyme,** in which the sound is close but not exact—*nerve / love; today / victory.*

Dickinson also often uses irony in her poems. **Irony** is the difference between what you expect to happen and what actually occurs. Dickinson's light tone is often an ironic comment on her serious subject matter.

Irony:

Man bites dog.

Reading Skill: Summarizing

When you **summarize** a text, you restate the main ideas in your own words, leaving out unimportant details. Summarizing the stanzas of Dickinson's poems can help you understand them.

Into the Poems

Emily Dickinson made up her own rules for her life—and for her poetry. While still a young woman, she became a recluse—staying at home and spending time with no one but her family. Only a few of her poems were published while she lived. She instructed her family to destroy her poems after her death. Fortunately for us, her request was not obeyed.

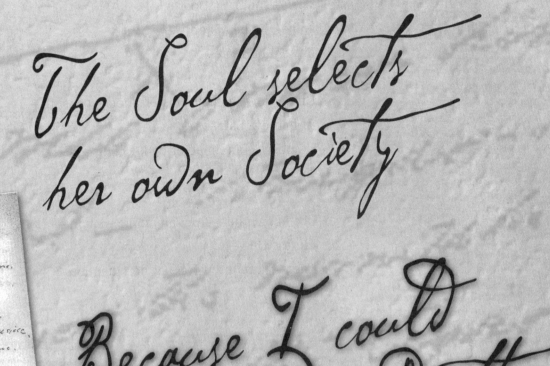

Emily Dickinson

The Soul selects her own Society

The Soul selects her own Society—
Then—shuts the Door—
To her divine Majority—
Present no more—

5   Unmoved—she notes the Chariots—pausing—
At her low Gate—
Unmoved—an Emperor be kneeling
Upon her Mat—

I've known her—from an ample[1] nation—
10 Choose One—
Then—close the Valves[2] of her attention—
Like Stone—

IN OTHER WORDS   The Soul is personified as a powerful woman, queen, or goddess. She refuses to open the door of her home to most of the people who come to see her. Sometimes she chooses to admit one of the many who stop at her gate, and then she shuts out all the others.

---

1. **ample:** more than enough.
2. **Valves:** opening in the membrane of the heart; faucet. Note: Dickinson's early editors changed the word *Valves* to *lids*.

"The Soul selects her own Society" from *The Poems of Emily Dickinson*, edited by Thomas H. Johnson. Copyright © 1951, 1955, 1979, 1983 by the President and Fellows of Harvard College. Published by The Belknap Press of Harvard University Press, Cambridge, Mass. Reproduced by permission of **Harvard University Press and the Trustees of Amherst College.**

Here's HOW

SLANT RHYME

In the first stanza, I see two sets of rhymes. *Door* and *more* are an exact rhyme because they sound exactly alike. *Society* and *Majority* are slant rhymes because their sound is close but not exact. The accented syllables have a different sound.

Your TURN

VOCABULARY

Majority can mean "the greater part of something," "having reached legal age," or (an older meaning) "superiority." Underline the meaning you think *majority* has in line 3.

Your TURN

SLANT RHYME

The two sets of rhymes in lines 5–8 are both the same kind. Are they exact or slant?

Here's HOW

SUMMARIZING

You can find a brief summary of the whole poem in the section titled "In Other Words."

Because I could not stop for Death

Because I could not stop for Death—
He kindly stopped for me—
The Carriage held but just Ourselves—
And Immortality.

5   We slowly drove—He knew no haste
And I had put away
My labor and my leisure too,
For His Civility[1]—

We passed the School, where Children strove[2]
10 At Recess—in the Ring—
We passed the Fields of Gazing Grain—
We passed the Setting Sun—

Or rather—He passed Us—
The Dews drew quivering and chill—
15 For only Gossamer,[3] my Gown—
My Tippet—only Tulle[4]—

We paused before a House that seemed
A Swelling of the Ground—
The Roof was scarcely visible—
20 The Cornice[5]—in the Ground—

Since then—'tis Centuries—and yet
Feels shorter than the Day
I first surmised[6] the Horses' Heads
Were toward Eternity—

---

1. **Civility** (suh VIL uh tee): politeness.
2. **strove** (strohv): tried hard.
3. **Gossamer** (GOS uh muhr): thin, soft material.
4. **Tippet . . . Tulle** (tool): shawl made of fine netting.
5. **Cornice** (KAWR nihs): projecting horizontal molding at the top of a building.
6. **surmised** (suhr MYZD): guessed; inferred.

Here's HOW

IRONY

I think there is an example of irony in line 2. We don't usually expect people to be glad when death comes, but the speaker of the poem says that death "kindly" stopped for her.

Your TURN

IRONY

Underlines words you think are ironic in lines 3–8, and explain the reasons for your choices on the lines below.

_____

_____

_____

_____

Your TURN

SUMMARIZING

The time period of this poem could be considered a day or a lifetime. Think about these possibilities as you summarize lines 9–12 in your own words on the lines below.

_____

_____

_____

_____

"Because I could not stop for Death" from *The Poems of Emily Dickinson,* edited by Thomas H. Johnson. Copyright © 1951, 1955, 1979 by the President and Fellows of Harvard College. Published by The Belknap Press of Harvard University Press, Cambridge, Mass. Reproduced by permission of **Harvard University Press and the Trustees of Amherst College.**

Summary Chart

When you **summarize,** you restate the main ideas in your own words. To increase your understanding of Emily Dickinson's poem "Because I could not stop for Death," write a summary of each stanza in the chart below. One has been done for you, but there is no one right answer.

"Because I could not stop for Death"

Stanza	Summary
1. Because I could not stop for Death— He kindly stopped for me— The Carriage held but just Ourselves— And Immortality.	
2. We slowly drove—He knew no haste And I had put away My labor and my leisure too, For His Civility—	
3. We passed the School, where Children strove At Recess—in the Ring— We passed the Fields of Gazing Grain— We passed the Setting Sun—	The speaker recalls her life—her childhood, her middle age, and her old age.
4. Or rather—He passed Us— The Dews drew quivering and chill— For only Gossamer, my Gown— My Tippet—only Tulle—	
5. We paused before a House that seemed A Swelling of the Ground— The Roof was scarcely visible— The Cornice—in the Ground—	
6. Since then—'tis Centuries—and yet Feels shorter than the Day I first surmised the Horses' Heads Were toward Eternity—	

The Rise of Realism: The Civil War to 1914

Based on the Student Edition text by Gary Q. Arpin

On the evening of April 12, 1861, the poet Walt Whitman attended the opera in Manhattan. Walking home, he heard the shouts of the newsboys and saw them dashing up the street. Whitman bought a copy of a newspaper and moved toward the streetlamps in front of a
5   hotel. There he read the news: Soldiers from the South had attacked Fort Sumter in the North. The U.S. Civil War had begun. Whitman would be one of the few American poets or writers to experience firsthand the greatest upheaval in United States history.

Slavery Divides the Country

10   What had brought the country to the point of civil war? Although there was more than one cause of the Civil War, slavery was at the heart of the conflict. The personal accounts of people who had been held in slavery—such as that of Frederick Douglass—revealed to the world the horrors and injustices of slavery. Many Northerners saw
15   slavery as going against the American ideals of equality. However, most Southerners did not want to do away with it. This difference caused emotions to run high on both sides of the issue. When violence erupted at Fort Sumter, the country plunged into civil war.

A Response to the War: Idealism

20   In Concord, Massachusetts—home of Ralph Waldo Emerson, Henry David Thoreau, Nathaniel Hawthorne, and many other intellectual leaders of the nation—a volunteer army quickly formed. The author and activist Ralph Waldo Emerson encouraged the young soldiers. He had long warned that war would come if slavery were not
25   abolished. Now he predicted that the war would be a long one. When the volunteers returned at summer's end, their spirits were low. They had lost the First Battle of Bull Run (July 1861), and many did not want to return to the front. But Emerson was convinced that the war must go on.

VOCABULARY

I know what my ideal day would be. I'd be swimming in a perfect lake. But what is *idealism* (line 19)? I checked a dictionary to be sure. *Idealism* is forming ideas of what is perfect or right and then trying to live by those ideas.

A Reality of the War: Appalling Suffering

Late in 1862, Walt Whitman went south to find and nurse his brother George, who had been wounded in battle. Whitman spent much of the war in Washington, D.C. He volunteered in a camp hospital, comforting the wounded and writing letters for them. Many soldiers were in very bad shape. Often they had been left on the battlefield for two or three days until the hospital could make room for them. Conditions were not very clean, and medicine was primitive. A major wound led to amputation[1] and even death.

In three years' time, Whitman visited thousands of wounded men. In his poems he had celebrated a vast, teeming[2] America. Now America passed before his eyes in the form of wounded men from every state. Still, Whitman remained hopeful. He praised the American soldier "with all his ways, his . . . dauntlessness, habits, practices, tastes, language, his fierce friendship, . . . his superb strength. . . ."

The Result of the War: Disillusionment

The same war that strengthened Whitman's hopefulness caused the writer Herman Melville's despair. Melville did not write a novel about the war, but he did write many poems about it. These poems are often dark and fearful. After the firing on Fort Sumter, for example, Melville wrote that while the young men looked forward to the war, their elders were filled with sorrow.

Melville based his poems on newspaper reports and battlefield visits. The poems record the heroism of both Southern and Northern soldiers as well as the uselessness of their efforts. But some of Melville's best war poems take an even bleaker turn. They suggest that at the core of humanity is not heroism or strength but evil.

The War in Literature

Aside from soldiers' letters, wartime diaries, and newspaper articles, notable literature from the Civil War period is rare. Why did such a major event produce such scant literature? One reason is that few major American writers saw the war firsthand. Emerson remained in Concord, knitting clothes for soldiers and writing patriotic lectures.

---

1. **amputation** (AM pyuh TAY shuhn): the cutting off of an arm or leg from the body.
2. **teeming** (TEEM ing): full of, crowded.

VOCABULARY

Appalling (line 30) means "shocking or horrible." In lines 35–38, underline three examples of appalling suffering.

VOCABULARY

I think I've found a word that means the opposite of *idealism*. It's *disillusionment* in line 45. The first sentence of the following paragraph tells me that we're dealing with contrasts—despair and hopefulness.

VOCABULARY

Read lines 57–60. Circle words that are clues to the meaning of *scant* in line 60. Then, write a brief definition of *scant* on the lines provided.

_____

_____

_____

Henry David Thoreau died in 1862, and Nathaniel Hawthorne died
two years later. Emily Dickinson stayed in Amherst, Massachusetts.
65 Many of the younger writers were abroad.

Another reason, though, is that the literary forms of the time were
not suited to express the horrors of war. The **realistic novel,** which
lent itself to harsh subject matter, had not yet come from Europe to
the United States. Thus, the great novel of the war, *The Red Badge of*
70 *Courage,* had to wait to be written. Its author, Stephen Crane, was not
born until six years after the war's end.

The Rise of Realism

Traditionally the **Romantic novel** had portrayed the adventures of
larger-than-life heroes. In this case, *romantic* refers to adventure, not
75 to love. James Fenimore Cooper's heroes, for example, execute brave
actions, daring chases, and exciting escapes.

Like Cooper, the major American writers of the mid-1800s
shunned[3] realism. Edgar Allan Poe, Nathaniel Hawthorne, and
Herman Melville used romance to express truths that realistic stories
80 could not contain.

After the Civil War, though, a new group of writers came of age.
These **realists** aimed to capture the details of ordinary life. Their gritty
subjects were drawn from the slums and factories of growing cities
and from the lives of realistic characters—poor factory workers,
85 dishonest politicians, even prostitutes.

Realism Takes Root in Europe

Realism had been around a long time in Europe before it emerged
in the United States. European writers embraced realism and wanted
to give readers a close, hard look at real life: how ordinary people
90 lived and dressed, what they thought, and what they talked about.
But realism went beyond wallpaper patterns, hairstyles, and
conversations. It also tried to explain *why* people behave the way they
do. New sciences such as biology, psychology, and sociology helped
realists explain the *why* of human behavior.

---

3. **shunned** (shuhnd): avoided.

VOCABULARY

When I tell my mother that I plan
to run a mile in three minutes, she
tells me to be realistic. She wants
me to face facts and look at what
is reasonable. So the *realistic
novel,* referred to in line 67, must
be about what *is,* not what we
wish could be.

VOCABULARY

The word *execute* (line 75)
can mean "administer," "put
to death," or "perform."
Underline the meaning it has
here.

VOCABULARY

In lines 87–93, underline
words that support the idea
that European writers
embraced, or eagerly took part
in, realistic writing.

Elements of Realism

95
- Rejection of the idealized, larger-than-life hero
- Detailed description of ordinary characters and events
- Emphasis on characters from cities and from lower classes
- Avoidance of the sensational and overly dramatic

100
- Use of everyday speech that reflects how people really speak
- Focus on ethical and social issues from real life

American Regionalism: Brush Strokes of Local Color

In America, realism had its roots in **regionalism.** Regionalism focuses on a particular region and the people who live there. American

105 regionalists include Kate Chopin, Harriet Beecher Stowe, and Bret Harte. These writers tried to create realistic portraits of the speech and manners of people in a certain region. However, their treatment of larger social conditions was often unrealistic.

Mark Twain succeeded as both a regionalist and a realist. He was

110 first known for his regional humor, but he later became famous for his satire.[4] His best novel, *Adventures of Huckleberry Finn* (1884), combines a biting picture of the injustices of pre–Civil War life with beautiful descriptions of the American landscape.

Realism and Naturalism: A Lens on Everyday Life

115 ■ "Smiling Realism"

The writer and editor William Dean Howells was a strong advocate[5] of realism. He insisted that it should deal with the lives of ordinary people, value characters over actions, and discuss important social questions. His "smiling realism" portrayed an America where people

120 may act foolishly but are basically good.

Other realistic novelists saw life as a harsher clash of forces. The Californian Frank Norris, for one, found Howells's fiction too strait-laced. Norris's writing is earthier, exploring the effects of large social forces on regular people. His novel *The Octopus* (1901), for example,

125 tells of the struggles between California farmers and the railroad companies. Like Harriet Beecher Stowe's antislavery novel, *Uncle Tom's Cabin* (1852), Norris's novels aimed at social change.

---

4. **satire** (SA TYR): literary work that makes fun of faults.
5. **advocate** (AD voh ket): person who speaks or writes in support of something.

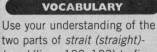

Use your understanding of the two parts of *strait (straight)-laced* (lines 122–123) to figure out what the word means. Then, write on the lines below what *strait-laced* tells you about Howells's fiction.

_____

_____

_____

_____

■ Grim Naturalism

Norris's brand of realism is known as **naturalism.** Naturalists tried to
130 dissect human behavior as objectively—without bias or prejudice—as
a scientist would. They believed that forces beyond people's control,
such as biology and the environment, make people act the way they
do. The naturalists tended to see life as a grim losing battle. Some saw
humans as victims who live crude lives, like animals that are slaves to
135 their instincts.

Elements of Naturalism

• Attempt to analyze human behavior scientifically

• Belief that human behavior is cause by inherited traits and by the
environment

140 • Sense that human beings cannot control their own future

• Sense that life is a losing battle

Psychological Realism: Inside the Human Mind

■ Exploring Motivation

New York's Henry James is considered America's greatest writer of
145 the psychological novel. His books are concerned with exploring
people's motivation—why they do what they do. James was also a
realist, but he did not agree with the naturalists that people are driven
mainly by their instincts. Instead, he believed that human motives are
rooted in the human mind. James placed his characters in complex
150 situations and then explored how they responded. Many of his novels
take place in Europe. An innocent, eager American confronts the
complex forces of European society and either defeats or is defeated
by them.

■ Examining Characters in Crisis

155 The novelist Stephen Crane was also intrigued by human psychology.
He preferred, though, to focus on moments of stress—the chaos of
the battlefield or a lifeboat lost at sea. Crane's work is often **ironic,**
placing human strains and struggles in the framework of a cold,

uncaring universe. Of all the nineteenth-century realists only Crane
160   could describe a stabbing death in this cool manner: "[The blade]
shot forward, and a human body, this citadel[6] of virtue, wisdom,
power, was pierced as easily as if it had been a melon." Crane's
combination of naturalism and irony made it finally possible to create
a true portrayal of the Civil War in literature.

165   Endings and Beginnings

The American nation experienced many changes between the Civil
War, and the outbreak of World War I. When the Civil War ended, in
1865, America was mostly a farming nation with little interest in other
nations. By the beginning of World War I, in 1914, the country was
170   driven by industry and international involvement. Between these two
wars, realism and naturalism dominated American literature. World
War I, however, would rock the world and shake people's faith in
humanity. The war would cause great changes in thought and faith.

---

6. citadel (SIT a del): fortress; fortified place; place of safety.

From Narrative of the Life of Frederick Douglass

Literary Focus: Metaphor

Writers and poets use **metaphors** to make creative comparisons without using specific words such as *like, as, than,* or *resembles*. You probably use and hear many metaphors in your daily life without realizing it. For example, when someone says that his grandmother gave him a big bear hug, which picture comes to mind?

A *bear hug* is a metaphor meaning a great big hug, such as a bear might give; it does not mean an actual hug given by a bear.

Reading Skill: Analyzing a Writer's Purpose

Writers use different kinds of writing to achieve their purposes. They might tell a story (narration), describe a scene (description), set forth the facts (exposition), or try to convince you of their point of view (persuasion). Persuasion is only one of the kinds of writing Frederick Douglass uses to convince readers of the horrors of slavery. As you read, notice what other kinds of writing he uses to achieve his purpose.

Into the Autobiography

Douglass was born a slave around 1817. His experience of the extreme cruelty of the slave system convinced him he had to be free. He escaped to the North when he was about twenty-one. From there he went to England, where friends bought his freedom. In 1847, Douglass returned to the United States and set up an antislavery newspaper. He also worked with the Underground Railroad helping people escape from slavery to the North.

FROM Narrative of the Life of Frederick Douglass

BASED ON THE AUTOBIOGRAPHY BY

Frederick Douglass

Here's HOW

ANALYZING A WRITER'S PURPOSE

In line 5, I think Douglass states directly the purpose of the story he is about to tell: He wrote the story to show how he got back his dignity and sense of self-worth.

Your TURN

ANALYZING A WRITER'S PURPOSE

In a narrative a writer usually tells about events in the order in which they happened. In lines 6–21, underline words and phrases that show when things happened.

The Battle with Mr. Covey

I have already hinted that the first six months of my stay at Mr. Covey's were much worse than the last. The events that brought about the change in Mr. Covey's attitude toward me are an important chapter in my humble history. I have told you how a man

5 was made a slave; now you will hear how a slave was made a man.

On one of the hottest days of the month of August 1833, Bill Smith, William Hughes, a slave named Eli, and myself were fanning wheat.[1] Hughes was clearing the fanned wheat from in front of the fan, Eli was turning the fan, Smith was feeding in the grain, and I was

10 carrying wheat to the fan. The work was simple, requiring strength rather than intellect; yet, to one not used to such work, it was very hard.

About three o'clock, my strength began to fail. I kept going as long as I could stagger to the fan's hopper, or bin, with the grain.

15 When I could no longer stand up, I fell down. Of course, the fan stopped. Everyone had his own work to do, and no one could do the work of another and his own at the same time.

Mr. Covey immediately came down from the house and wanted to know what was the matter. Bill answered that I was sick, and there

20 was no one to bring the wheat to the fan. I had crawled under the fence to get out of the sun.

Mr. Covey came over, gave me a savage kick in the side, and told me to get up. I managed to get up and stagger to the grain tub but fell down again. Mr. Covey picked up a piece of wood, hit me on the

25 head, and again told me to get up. Blood was running from the wound on my head. I decided to run away, tell my master what had happened, and ask his protection. I waited until Covey wasn't looking and headed for the woods. When Covey noticed, he yelled at me, threatening what he would do if I did not come back. I paid no

30 attention and kept on going.

I had not gone far before what little strength I had failed me, and I fell down. After a while, I nerved myself up[2] again and started on my way. It took me five hours to walk seven miles. At last, I

---

1. **fanning wheat:** separating usable grain.
2. **nerved myself up:** got my strength and confidence back.

arrived at my master's store. My appearance should have melted
35 even a heart of iron. From the top of my head to my feet, I was
covered with blood. My hair was all clotted with dust and blood;
my shirt was stiff with blood. My legs and feet were torn bloody by
briers and thorns. I looked like a man who had barely escaped a den
of wild beasts.

40   In this bloody state I stood before my master. I begged him for
protection, and I told him I wanted him to get me a new home. I said
that Covey would surely kill me if I stayed with him.

        Master Thomas ridiculed the idea that there was any danger of
Mr. Covey's killing me. He said that he would not think of taking me
45 away from Covey because he would lose the whole year's wages I
would earn for him. He said that I belonged to Mr. Covey for one
year, and if I did not go back, he would whip me.

        I started off to Covey's the next morning. As I was climbing
over the fence to Covey's fields, out ran Covey with his whip. I turned
50 and ran back to the woods.

        That night I met up with Sandy Jenkins, a slave that I knew. I told
him my troubles, we talked the matter over, and I got his advice as to
what to do. Sandy told me that I must go back to Covey; but that
before I went, I must go with Sandy into the woods where a certain
55 root grew. I was to take some of that root with me, always carrying it
on my right side. The root would make it impossible for Mr. Covey, or
any other white man, to whip me. At first I rejected the idea, thinking
that simply carrying a root in my pocket would not protect me. Sandy
told me it could do no harm, so to please him, I finally took the root
60 and, according to his direction, carried it on my right side. This was
Sunday morning.

        I started for home, and as I walked through the gate, out came
Mr. Covey on his way to church. He spoke to me kindly, gave me an
easy chore, and went on his way. Now, Mr. Covey's strange conduct
65 made me begin to think that maybe there was something in the root
that Sandy had given me. All went well till Monday morning. On this
morning the power of the root was fully tested.

ANALYZING A WRITER'S PURPOSE

Lines 34–39 describe Douglass's appearance after he was beaten and walked seven miles. What do you think his purpose is in writing this description?

_____

_____

_____

_____

_____

Here's HOW

METAPHOR

I notice a metaphor in lines 34–35 when Douglass says that the way he looks would melt "a heart of iron." I don't think Douglass means that a real metal heart would melt. Instead, he is saying that even a mean, uncaring person would feel sympathy.

NARRATIVE OF THE LIFE OF FREDERICK DOUGLASS

ANALYZING A WRITER'S PURPOSE

Douglass admits in lines 70–71 that he doesn't know where he got the idea to fight back. What is the purpose of this description of his state of mind?

_____

_____

_____

Here's HOW

METAPHOR

In line 87, Douglass says his fight with Mr. Covey "relit the dying embers of freedom." I don't think he means that freedom itself was like a fire that was dying out. Instead, he means that he had given up his desire for freedom, but now his desire has been revived.

METAPHOR

Circle the metaphor in line 91. Then, describe what it means.

_____

_____

_____

Long before daylight, I was called out to rub, curry,[3] and feed the horses. While I was doing this, Mr. Covey came in, knocked me
70 down, and started to tie me up. Suddenly—and where the idea came from, I do not know—I decided to fight back. I grabbed Covey by the throat and held on to him. Covey soon called out to Hughes for help. Hughes came and grabbed hold of me. I gave him a hard kick and he let go. Covey dragged me over to a stick that was lying outside
75 the stable door. As he was leaning over to get the stick, I jumped up and threw him to the ground.

By this time, Bill came over, and Covey yelled, "Take hold of him, take hold of him!" Bill refused, saying he had been hired out to work, and not to whip me. He left Covey and me to fight it out, and we
80 were at it for nearly two hours. Finally Covey let me go, puffing and blowing, saying that if I had not fought back, he would not have whipped me half so much. The truth was, he had not whipped me at all. He got the worst of the bargain[4]—he had drawn no blood from me, but I had made him bleed. For the rest of the six months that I
85 was with Mr. Covey, he never again laid a finger on me.

The battle with Mr. Covey was the turning point in my life as a slave. It relit the dying embers of freedom and revived my sense of manhood. It brought back my self-confidence and again inspired me with a determination to be free. My feeling of triumph made up for
90 whatever else might come to me, even death. Only someone who has suffered under the bloody arm of slavery can understand how I felt. I felt as I never felt before. My spirit rose, cowardice left me, and bold defiance took its place. I resolved that, however long I might remain a slave in form, the day had passed forever when I was a
95 slave in fact.

---

3. **curry** (KUR ee): to rub and clean a horse.
4. **got the worst of the bargain:** lost. Covey and Douglass agreed to fight. At the end, Covey was bleeding, but Douglass was not.

Metaphor Chart

Metaphors involve imaginative comparisons of two things that do not seem at all alike. To be sure you understand the metaphors in "The Narrative of the Life of Frederick Douglass," complete the chart below.

Metaphors from Douglass's autobiography are listed in the left-hand column of the chart. In the middle column, write down the two things that are being compared. In the right-hand column, explain what the metaphor means. One has been done for you.

Metaphor	Comparison	Meaning
1. "My appearance should have melted even a heart of iron." (lines 34–35)		
2. "It relit the dying embers of freedom" (line 87)	Freedom is compared to a fire.	The fight gave Douglass back his great desire for freedom, which had almost died out.
3. "Only someone who has suffered under the bloody arm of slavery can understand" (lines 90–91)		

A Mystery of Heroism

Literary Focus: Situational Irony

If your local TV news station reported a story about a fire station that burned down, the reporter might call it an **ironic situation.** You wouldn't expect a fire station to burn down. Irony also takes place in literature. A situation that turns out to be very different from, or even opposite to, what was expected is called **situational irony.**

Situational Irony

Well now, this is unexpected!

Reading Skill: Summarizing

A good way to increase your understanding of a story is to summarize passages. When you **summarize,** you restate the author's points in your own words. You leave out the details and tell only the main points. Summarizing every page will help you follow the most important action and ideas of a story.

Into the Story

Many war stories focus on the military leaders. But the author of "A Mystery of Heroism," Stephen Crane, was more interested in the foot soldier than in the officers. This may be why Crane was so popular with readers. Ironically, Crane himself never fought in a war. He was born after the Civil War had ended.

A Mystery of Heroism

BASED ON THE SHORT STORY BY

Stephen Crane

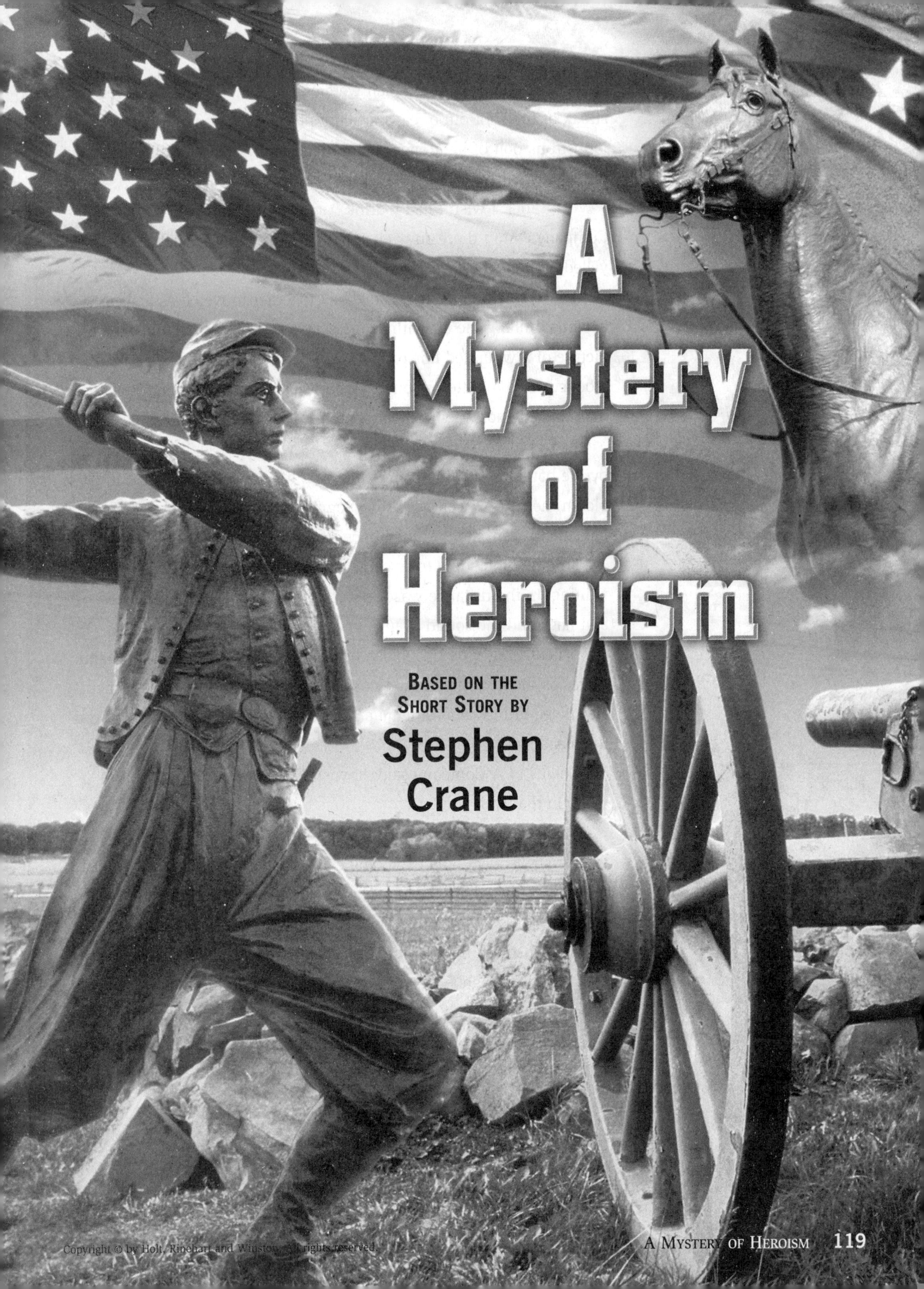

The dark uniforms of the men were coated with dust. A thick red streak of fire shot out of each artillery piece[1] as it was fired, like a monstrous bolt of lightning. The artillerymen ran about, following the orders of their officers.

5   "Thunder, I wish I had a drink," said Fred Collins of A Company. "Ain't there any water round here?" Then somebody yelled, "There goes the bugler!"[2]

     The eyes of the soldiers moved all together to watch as a shell exploded, filling the air with shafts of flame. There was an instant

10 picture of a wounded horse leaping and a rider leaning back with a crooked arm. A glittering bugle swung clear of the rider's back as the man and the horse fell. The air smelled like fire.

     Across a pretty stretch of green grass was a house, half destroyed by the battle and by men chopping it up for firewood. A shell had

15 blown the nearby well house[3] to fragments, and lines of gray smoke indicated where the barn had once stood.

     From behind some trees came a sound like two huge animals fighting. In the distance was the sight of swift-moving men, horses, and flags and the sound of men cheering wildly.

20   A lieutenant rode up slowly, holding his right arm in his left hand. It was as though this arm did not belong to him, but to another man. He smiled grimly when the men stared at him, and he rode off toward the meadow.

     Collins of A Company said: "I wish I had a drink. I bet there's

25 water in that well yonder!"

     "Yes," someone answered, "but how you goin' to get it?"

     For shells were now exploding everywhere, including in the little meadow. Brown earth was flung in huge handfuls, and the young blades of grass were being massacred.

30   A shell struck the gray ruins of the house, and the shattered wall fell in fragments. One of the artillery units on the hill was also attacked, and through the smoke and dust white legs could be seen stretched out on the ground. Even the horses that pulled the canons

---

1. **artillery piece:** cannon.
2. **bugler:** person who sounds the "charge" or "retreat" signal on a bugle.
3. **well house:** small building that contains a water well.

were hit by the fiery shells as they waited patiently. One bleeding
35 horse raised its nose to heaven.

Off in the meadow the wounded officer who had held one arm
in the other now lay motionless in the meadow, and all around him
angry shells flew.

Some comrades of Collins teased him, saying, "Well, if you
40 want a drink so bad, why don't you go get it?"

"Well, I will in a minute," cried Collins, "if you don't shut up."

"Sure," another man jeered.[5] "You'll run right through that
meadow, won't you?"

Collins frowned and went to find his captain, who was talking
45 with the colonel of the regiment.

"Captain," said Collins, standing at attention, "I want permission
to go get some water from that well over yonder."

The captain and the colonel turned and looked across the
meadow. "You must be pretty thirsty, Collins?" laughed the captain.
50 "Yes, sir; I am," said Collins.

"Well," said the captain, "can't you wait?"

"No, sir," said Collins.

"Don't you think that's a big risk for a drink of water?" said the
colonel.
55 "I dunno whether 'tis," said Collins.

"Well," said the colonel, "If you want to go, go. Take some of the
other boys' canteens with you, and hurry back."

"Yes, sir," said Collins.

Collins's friends could hardly believe he was going to do it, but
60 he walked away from them, swinging five or six canteens by their
cords.

As he walked, Collins knew he was walking squarely into the
face of death. But he was not sure that he would go back even if
he could. He was mainly amazed that he had allowed his mind to
65 maneuver[6] his body into this situation.

He wondered why he didn't feel afraid. If being fearless made
him a hero, he was disappointed to realize that heroes were
not much. No, he could not be a hero, because heroes were perfect.

---

5. **jeered:** taunted, made fun of.
6. **maneuver:** move.

Your TURN

SUMMARIZING

Re-read lines 39–58. In two or three sentences, summarize what happens in this passage.

_____

_____

_____

_____

_____

_____

_____

Your TURN

SITUATIONAL IRONY

What surprises you about Collins's decision to go get water?

_____

_____

_____

_____

_____

_____

_____

_____

Collins doesn't really become afraid until he reaches the water that he wanted so badly (lines 78–79). I expected him to feel relief when he reached the well.

Your
TURN

Re-read lines 95–97. What is the overall irony of this story?

_____

_____

_____

_____

_____

_____

_____

_____

_____

_____

70 He was not perfect. He had borrowed money from a friend and then avoided his friend for ten months. Also, when his mother had wanted him to work on the farm, he had been irritable[7] and childish and had behaved badly. His mother had died since he had come to the war.

As he walked toward the well, he was suddenly surrounded by what seemed to be flying arrows, flaming red. Little pieces of hot 75 shell howled through the air around him. He made a mad rush for the house, knocking the canteens together as he ran.

He flung himself down, peered into the darkness of the well, and started to fill the canteens. Suddenly, he was terrified, as the canteens filled with maddening slowness. When a shell exploded 80 nearby, filling the well with pink light, he dropped the canteens and picked up the old well bucket. He quickly filled it with water and started to carry it back across the meadow, spilling some as he ran awkwardly. All around him screamed angels of death.

Before him was the officer with the shattered arm. He was still 85 alive, and he raised up, his face white with pain. He spoke: "Say, young man, give me a drink of water, will you?"

"I can't," screamed Collins. He started to run away, but then he came back. "Here it is!" he cried. "Here it is!"

His shaking hands caused the water to splash all over the face 90 of the dying man. Then he ran on, back to his regiment, where the captain waved the bucket away and told him to give it to the men.

Two laughing young lieutenants were the first to take the bucket. They each tugged at it, as one cried, "Don't, Billie! You'll make me spill it."

95 Suddenly they cried out, and there was the thud of the wooden bucket on the ground. The two lieutenants glared at each other. The bucket lay on the ground empty.

_____

7. irritable: easy to annoy.

Situational Irony

Situational irony occurs when there is a difference between what is expected and what actually happens. To better understand situational irony in this story, complete the chart below. The left-hand column contains what we might expect to happen in a story of wartime heroism. In the right-hand column, fill in what actually occurs in "A Mystery of Heroism." One item is completed for you.

What We Expect	What Happens in the Story
1. Courage comes through sacrificing personal desires for the good of a group.	Collins's motive is selfish. He wants the water because he is thirsty.
2. The hero does what he thinks is right. He doesn't care what other people think of him.	
3. The hero has a clear sense of purpose.	
4. People are grateful for other people's sacrifices.	

The Gettysburg Address

Literary Focus: Speech

In giving a speech, the first thing you want to do is hold your listeners' attention. You do this by speaking loudly, clearly, and with expression. But you also need a well-written speech to begin with. The Gettysburg Address is considered one of the best speeches ever written. It is still read and admired today for the importance of its ideas, the beauty of its language, and its clarity and brevity.

Reading Skill: Analyzing a Writer's Style

Writers use certain elements of style to make their speeches interesting and memorable. For example, they might pay special attention to:

- **Word choice.** The words a writer chooses will help determine the **tone** of the speech—whether it is serious or humorous, for example.
- **Parallelism.** The repetition of phrases or sentences in the same grammatical structure helps make the argument of the speech clear and easy to follow. A good example of parallelism is found in Patrick Henry's statement "Give me liberty, or give me death!"
- **Repetition.** Repeating words and ideas plants them more firmly in the listeners' minds.

As you read his famous speech, notice how Abraham Lincoln uses these elements of style to make his point.

Into the Speech

Gettysburg was the greatest battle of the Civil War and its turning point. Fought on July 1–3, 1863, it left 5,660 dead, 27,000 wounded, and 10,500 missing. A few months later, on November 19, 1863, Lincoln spoke at the dedication of a memorial cemetery in Gettysburg, Pennsylvania.

The Gettysburg Address

Abraham Lincoln

THE GETTYSBURG ADDRESS **125**

Fourscore and seven[1] years ago our fathers brought forth on this continent a new nation, conceived[2] in Liberty, and dedicated to the proposition that all men are created equal.

Now we are engaged in a great civil war, testing whether that
5   nation, or any nation so conceived and so dedicated, can long endure. We are met on a great battlefield of that war. We have come to dedicate a portion of that field as a final resting place for those who here gave their lives that that nation might live. It is altogether fitting and proper that we should do this.

IN OTHER WORDS   Eighty-seven years ago, our founding fathers formed a new nation, based on the ideas of liberty and equality.

Now we are fighting a great civil war, testing whether such a nation can last. We meet on a battlefield of that war to establish a cemetery for those who died fighting for their country's survival. It is right that we do this.

10   But, in a larger sense, we cannot dedicate—we cannot consecrate[3]—we cannot hallow[4]—this ground. The brave men, living and dead, who struggled here, have consecrated it far above our poor power to add or detract. The world will little note nor long remember what we say here, but it can never forget what they did here. It is for
15   us the living, rather, to be dedicated here to the unfinished work which they who fought here have thus far so nobly advanced. It is rather for us to be here dedicated to the great task remaining before us—that from these honored dead we take increased devotion to that cause for which they gave the last full measure of devotion—that we
20   here highly resolve that these dead shall not have died in vain—that this nation, under God, shall have a new birth of freedom—and that

---

1. **fourscore and seven:** eighty-seven. A score is twenty. The Declaration of Independence was signed in 1776. Lincoln is speaking 87 years later, in 1863.
2. **conceived** *v.* used as *adj.:* developed; imagined.
3. **consecrate** *v.:* set apart as sacred or holy.
4. **hallow** *v.:* make holy.

government of the people, by the people, for the people, shall not perish from the earth.

IN OTHER WORDS But really, we cannot make this ground holy. The men who fought and died here have already done that. The world won't remember what we say here, but it will never forget what those brave men did. It is our job to finish what they began, so that they will not have died without reason. We must make sure that our freedom and democracy will survive.

Your TURN

ANALYZING A WRITER'S STYLE

Underline the parallelisms in line 22. This is one of the most famous parts of the speech. Why do you think Lincoln chose these phrases instead of simply saying "democracy"?

_____
_____
_____
_____
_____
_____
_____
_____
_____
_____

Style Chart

In writing a good speech, a writer is likely to use these elements of style:

- **word choice**—the words chosen determine the tone
- **parallelism**—repetition of the same grammatical structure
- **repetition**—use of the same words and ideas over and over

These elements are listed in the left-hand column of the chart below. For each one, an example is given from "The Gettysburg Address." In the extra space, add one or two other examples from the speech. Then, in the right-hand column, tell what each example adds to the speech. One has been done for you.

Element of Style	Contribution to the Speech
1. Word choice: "proposition" (line 3)	This legal-sounding word gives a serious tone.
2. Parallelism: "we cannot dedicate— we cannot consecrate—we cannot hallow" (lines 10–11)	
3. Repetition: "dedicate" or "dedicated" is used six times (lines 2, 5, 7, 10, 15, and 17)	

Vocabulary Development

Developing Vocabulary

Read the definition of each word below. Then, write an original sentence of your own using that word. Include in your sentence clues to the meaning of the word. One has been done for you.

1. fourscore and seven (line 1): eighty-seven. A score is twenty.

My grandmother is really old; she is fourscore and seven!

2. conceived (line 2) *v.* used as *adj.*: developed; imagined.

3. consecrate (line 11) *v.*: set apart as sacred or holy.

4. hallow (line 11) *v.*: make holy.

To Build a Fire

Literary Focus: Naturalism

Naturalists were writers who tried to show life exactly as it is. These writers tried to look at life unemotionally—to write down on paper exactly what a photographer would capture on film. Nature is a common subject for the naturalist. But the naturalist's view of nature is very different from the Romantic's. When Romantics looked at nature, they saw a source of beauty and inspiration. When naturalists looked at nature, they saw great power and wild forces beyond human control.

Reading Skill: Analyzing Cause and Effect

When you push a ball, it rolls. The push is the **cause.** The rolling action is the **effect** of the push. The plot of a story is made up of a string of causes and effects. One event causes another, which causes another. Understanding cause and effect helps you understand *why* things happen in a story. As you read, you might want to make a chart like the one below to keep track of causes and their effects.

Cause	Effect
The temperature was −50°.	The man's spit froze in the air.

Into the Story

The Yukon River valley in northwestern Canada was a wilderness until 1896. Then gold was discovered there. Soon thousands moved there to get rich quickly. Jack London learned about the area and the people it attracted when he went there to search for gold. Many of the people who rushed to the region were unaware of the dangers of the very cold climate. Furthermore, they had no experience living in the wilderness.

To Build a Fire

BASED ON THE SHORT STORY BY
Jack London

Your TURN

ANALYZING CAUSE AND EFFECT

Lines 12–13 say "The trouble with him was that he lacked imagination." How might this lack of imagination cause a bad effect?

_____

_____

_____

Here's HOW

NATURALISM

In lines 18–19, nature is warning this guy to be careful. His spit freezes in midair!

Your TURN

NATURALISM

In lines 25–30, underline the words that show that the dog understands nature's message better than the man does.

Day had broken gray and very cold when the man turned off the Yukon trail onto a little-traveled trail. He climbed the high earth bank, and at the top he stopped to catch his breath and look at his watch. It was nine in the morning on a clear day, but he could not
5   see the sun. He had not seen the sun in several days.

The man looked back the way he had come. The Yukon River lay a mile wide and hidden under three feet of ice. On top of this ice were as many feet of snow. North and south, as far as his eye could see, was unbroken white, except for a dark line that was the trail.

10   The absence of the sun, the tremendous cold, the strangeness of it all had no effect on the man. He was a newcomer to this land, and this was his first winter. The trouble with him was that he lacked imagination. He noticed things without understanding their significance.[1] He knew that 50 degrees below zero was very cold,
15   but that fact did not lead him to think about man's frailty[2] or his place in the universe. In such weather a man must dress warmly, but that there should be more to it than that did not enter his head.

As he turned to go on, he spat and was startled by a sharp, explosive crackle. He spat again, and the spittle crackled in the air.
20   Undoubtedly it was colder than 50 below, but that did not matter. He was headed to a camp where he knew his friends were waiting. He would be there by six, a bit after dark, but they would have a fire going and supper would be ready. Under his shirt he had biscuits and bacon for his lunch.

25   The trail he followed was faint because a foot of snow had fallen since the last sled had passed over the trail. A dog, a big native husky, trotted at the man's side. Although it knew nothing about temperatures, its instinct[3] told the dog how cold it really was—not 50, or even 60 below zero, but 75. The cold depressed the dog. It wanted
30   the man to stop and make camp or build a fire.

Frozen moisture from their breathing settled on the man's beard and the dog's muzzle. Once in a while the man thought about how very cold it was. He had never experienced such cold.

The man held on through several miles of woods. He crossed a

---

1. **significance** (sihg NIH fih kuhns): importance.
2. **frailty** (FRAY uhl tee): weakness.
3. **instinct** (IHN stihngt): natural ability; inherited, not learned behavior.

35 wide, flat area and dropped down to a small stream, Henderson
Creek. He saw by his watch that it was ten o'clock, and he knew that
he was ten miles from the forks.[4] He was making four miles an hour,
and he figured that he would arrive at the forks at half-past noon.

He kept rubbing his cheeks and his nose with his mittens, and as
40 soon as he stopped rubbing, they were numb[5] again. He knew frosted
cheeks were a bit painful, but never serious.

The man was still very observant.[6] He knew that in some places
springs bubbled up from the ground and, under the snow, there
would be icy water where a man could sink up to his waist. He
45 came across several such traps, which had a sunken appearance.
Once he had a very close call. Suspecting danger, he ordered the
dog to go in front, but the dog did not want to go. It hung back until
the man shoved it forward, and then it went quickly across the
unbroken, white surface. Suddenly it broke through, struggled to
50 one side, and escaped to firmer footing. It had wet its forefeet and
legs, and almost immediately the water that clung to the dog turned
to ice. Acting on instinct, the dog bit the ice away from between his
toes. The man took off a mitten and helped the dog free his paws of
the ice. In less than a minute the man's exposed fingers grew
55 numb.

At half past twelve the man arrived at the forks in the creek. He
took his lunch from under his shirt and sat on a log to eat.
Immediately he felt the numbness creeping into his hands and feet.
He had forgotten to build a fire. A bit frightened, he stood and
60 stamped his feet until the feeling returned. It certainly was cold, he
thought.

To warm himself, he walked up and down, stamping his feet and
swinging his arms. Then he got out his matches and started to make a
fire, finding twigs and firewood, and soon he had a roaring blaze. He
65 ate his biscuits. For the moment he had outwitted the cold. The dog
stretched out in front of the fire, close enough to enjoy the warmth
but far enough away not to burn his fur.

---

4. **forks:** the place where a road, path, river, etc., divides or branches.
5. **numb** (nuhm): without any physical feeling.
6. **observant** (uhb ZUHR vuhnt): noticing.

Here's
HOW

NATURALISM

In lines 68–72, the dog shows again that his instincts are closer to nature than the man's. The dog knows the extreme cold is a problem.

Your
TURN

VOCABULARY

The term *old-timer* in line 81 is made up of two smaller words. Without the hyphen an *old timer* might mean an "old clock." Add the hyphen, and the words together have another meaning. Write that meaning on the lines below. Use context clues or a dictionary for help.

_____

_____

_____

_____

Here's
HOW

NATURALISM

The tone in lines 85–89 worries me. This guy is too pleased with himself just for building a fire. I think nature will win in the end.

After eating, the man started walking again up the trail. The dog wanted desperately to go back to the fire. It knew about cold in a way
70 the man did not, and it understood that it was not good to walk in such fearful cold. It was best to lie snug in a hole in the snow. But the man whistled, and the dog swung in at the man's heels and followed after.

And then it happened. Suddenly the man crashed through a crust of snow into icy water halfway to his knees. He cursed his
75 luck, for he would have to stop again and build a fire to dry his feet and his shoes and socks.

He found dry twigs and sticks and some dry grass, and he worked slowly and carefully. Gradually the fire grew as he put larger pieces of wood onto it. He knew there must be no failure. When it is
80 75 below zero, a man must not fail in his first attempt to build a fire, especially when his feet are wet. The old-timer on Sulfur Creek had warned him, and now he appreciated the advice. His hands were numb, and his face and his feet were numb also. Now that he was not walking, he felt cold all over.

85 But he was safe, for the fire was a success. Remembering the old-timer's advice, never to travel alone on a day this cold, he smiled. Well, here he was; he had had the accident; he was alone; and he had saved himself. Any man who was a man could travel alone. As long as he kept his head, he would be all right. The fire
90 snapped and crackled, but before he could take off his shoes to dry them, it happened. He had built his roaring fire under a tree and now, from the branches above, an avalanche[7] of heavy snow fell. The fire was no more. The man was shocked. He feared he had just heard his own death sentence. For a moment he stared at the spot where the
95 fire had been, and then he grew very calm. He would make a new fire, but he realized that even if he succeeded he would most likely lose some toes.

He gathered more dry grass and twigs, but his fingers could not grip them, and he had to grab whole handfuls. He grabbed some
100 rotten twigs and green moss along with the dry twigs. All the while the dog watched, yearning for a new fire.

---

7. **avalanche** (A vuh LANCH): a moving mass; a sudden great rush.

When the twigs and grass were ready, the man reached into his pocket, but now his fingers were completely numb. He fought back panic as he beat his hands on his body to try to get back some

105 feeling. He got his matches from his pocket, but he dropped them all in the snow. He tried to pick them up, but he couldn't. He scooped some matches, along with a large quantity of snow, into his lap. He could not pick them up with his useless hands, but he managed to take one match between his teeth and, after trying twenty times to

110 strike it against his pant leg, he succeeded, but the match fell into the snow and went out. In a moment of despair, he knew that the old-timer was right; after fifty below a man should travel with a partner.

He took a whole bunch of matches between the heels of both

115 hands and managed to light them all at once, seventy wooden matches all at once! He held the blaze to a piece of birch bark, but he could smell the flesh of his hands burning. In spite of the pain, he did not drop the matches. He was shivering now, as he awkwardly put pieces of twig onto the flames. A piece of green moss fell on the

120 feeble[8] fire, and when he awkwardly tried to poke it away, the flames died.

He looked over at the dog, sitting across the ruins of the fire from him, and a wild idea came into his head. He remembered the tale of the man, caught in a blizzard, who killed a steer and crawled inside

125 the carcass[9] to stay warm. He would kill the dog and bury his hands in the warm body. Then he could build another fire. He spoke to the dog, calling it towards him, but something in his voice frightened the animal, and it stayed where it was.

Struggling to stay calm, he got up onto his feet and looked down

130 to be sure he was standing, for he could not feel his feet. He lunged[10] for the dog and caught hold of it. He wanted to kill the animal, but his numb hands could not strangle it, nor could he draw his knife. He let it go, and it ran off snarling with its tail between its legs, to watch him from forty feet away. The man beat his hands against his body

135 but had no feeling in them.

---

8. **feeble** (FEE buhl): weak.
9. **carcass** (KAHR kuhs): dead body.
10. **lunged** (luhnjd): moved forward suddenly.

Here's HOW

ANALYZING CAUSE AND EFFECT

Every time this guy does anything, he messes it up. Look at lines 105–107. Dropping the matches is going to cause big problems.

Your TURN

ANALYZING CAUSE AND EFFECT

In lines 114–121, the man has succeeded in lighting a bunch of wooden matches, but his hands are still cold and clumsy. In this paragraph, underline the effect that this clumsiness causes.

Your TURN

NATURALISM

In lines 122–128, the dog shows again that its instincts are closer to nature than man's. What does the dog do that proves this? Write your answer on the lines below:

_____

_____

_____

_____

_____

Your TURN

ANALYZING CAUSE AND EFFECT

How does the man's acceptance of death in lines 148–151 affect his behavior? Write your answer on the lines below.

_____

_____

_____

_____

Your TURN

NATURALISM

Too late the man finally realizes that the old-timer was right (line 155). What is London's message here?

_____

_____

_____

_____

_____

_____

_____

He quickly realized that this was no longer a matter of freezing his fingers and toes; it was a matter of life and death, with the chances against him. He panicked, and he began to run up the trail, but he soon grew weak and stumbled. He tried to get up, but he

140 failed. He decided to sit and rest before he tried to walk some more. As he sat and got his breath back, he noticed that he had stopped shivering. He now felt warm and comfortable. Before long, however, he thought of freezing totally, and so he got up to run again, with the dog at his heels. It angered him that the dog seemed so warm and

145 safe in this frozen world.

He was losing this battle with the frost. It was creeping into his body from all sides. He ran another hundred feet and then fell face down in the snow. It was his last panic. He finally sat up and now thought only of meeting death with dignity. He felt drowsy, and sleep

150 seemed a good idea; he could die in his sleep. Freezing was not so bad as people thought. There were lots worse ways to die.

He pictured the boys finding his body the next day. It certainly was cold, he thought. When he got back to the States, he could tell the folks what real cold was. He thought of the old man at Sulfur

155 Creek and said, "You were right, old-timer."

Then the man drifted off into the most comfortable and satisfying sleep he had ever known. The dog sat facing him and waiting. The brief day drew to a close in a long, slow twilight. The dog whined, but the man remained silent. Later, the dog whined loudly. Still later,

160 it crept close to the man and caught the smell of death. This made the animal bristle and back away. It waited a little longer, howling under a cold sky full of bright stars. Then it turned and trotted up the trail in the direction of the camp it knew, where it would find the other food providers and fire providers.

136   HOLT ADAPTED READER

Cause and Effect

You can think of **cause** and **effect** in a story like beads on a necklace. Each "cause bead" is followed by at least one "effect bead." The whole necklace (story) is made up of beads (actions) that are linked together.

When you understand cause and effect, you understand *why* things happen in a story. To explore cause and effect in "To Build a Fire," use the graphic below. One cause and its effect have already been done for you.

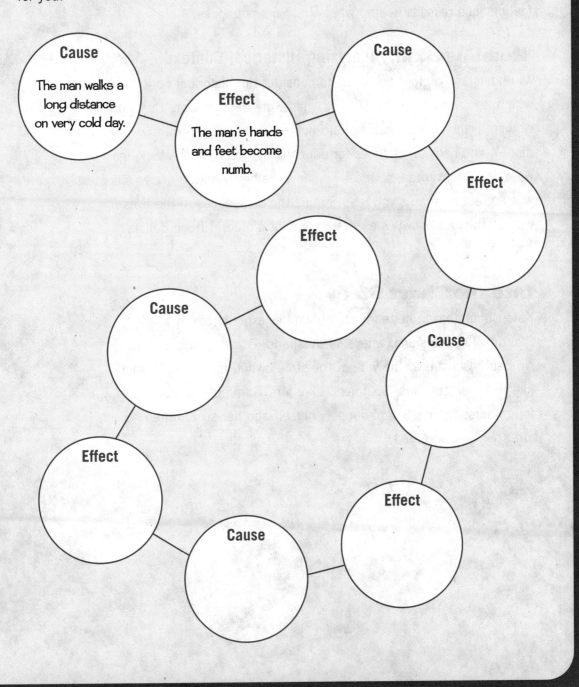

A Pair of Silk Stockings

Literary Focus: Motivation

When you ask *why* a character does something, you are asking about motivation. **Motivation** refers to the reasons for a character's action. As in life, characters in a story often have complicated motives for what they do. As you read "A Pair of Silk Stockings," look for the feelings and reasons behind what Mrs. Sommers does.

Reading Skill: Analyzing Historical Context

To understand a story, you need to consider the historical period in which it is written. In the 1890s, when Kate Chopin wrote this story, women in the United States could not vote, did not control their own money, and had few chances for education or jobs. Nylon stockings were not yet invented, so most women wore heavy cotton ones—silk was a great luxury. As you read, notice the differences in the lives of women then and now. One difference is how much fifteen dollars could buy.

Into the Short Story

Kate Chopin based her early stories on her experiences in Cloutierville, Louisiana, where her husband, Oscar, owned a store. No doubt Chopin, as the wife of the store owner, met many women like her character Mrs. Sommers. Like Mrs. Sommers, Chopin found herself struggling to support herself and her six children after her husband died.

A Pair of Silk Stockings

BASED ON THE SHORT STORY BY
Kate Chopin

Here's
HOW

MOTIVATION

I notice in lines 1–5 that Mrs. Sommers takes days to decide how to spend her extra money. I would guess the reason is that she is poor, so she wants to get the most for her money.

Here's
HOW

ANALYZING HISTORICAL CONTEXT

In lines 6–13, I see that Mrs. Sommers can get a lot for fifteen dollars, but what she chooses is really different from what my mom would buy. Most people don't make their own shirts today. They'd probably buy new ones instead of patching them.

Your
TURN

ANALYZING HISTORICAL CONTEXT

Underline the details in lines 20–32 that show what life was like for a woman in Mrs. Sommers's day. How is her life similar to or different from a woman's life today?

_____

_____

_____

_____

_____

_____

One day little Mrs. Sommers found she had an extra fifteen dollars.[1] The bulge it caused in her purse made her feel unusually important. For days she thought about how to spend the money. She did not wish to act hastily, to do anything she might afterward

5 regret.

During a restless night she decided to spend an extra dollar or two for Janie's shoes, so they would last longer. She'd buy yards of cloth for new shirts for the children instead of patching the old shirts. Mag should have a new dress, and still there would be enough for

10 new stockings—two pairs apiece—and what darning[2] that would save! She would buy caps for the boys and sailor hats for the girls. The vision of her children looking fresh and dainty and new for once in their lives excited her.

The neighbors sometimes talked of "better days" that little

15 Mrs. Sommers had known before she ever thought of being Mrs. Sommers. She herself had no time—not one second to think about the past. The present kept her busy. A vision of the future as a gaunt[3] monster sometimes scared her, but luckily tomorrow never comes.

20 Mrs. Sommers knew the value of bargains, and she could fight the crowds for them and wait patiently to be served. But that day she was a little faint and tired because she had forgotten to eat lunch. Feeling limp, she rested her hand aimlessly upon the counter. She gradually realized that she was touching something

25 very soothing. Her hand lay upon a pile of silk stockings. A sign announced that their price had been reduced from two dollars and fifty cents to one dollar and ninety-eight cents. A young girl behind the counter offered to show her the silk hosiery. Mrs. Sommers smiled, just as if she had been asked to inspect a tiara[4] of diamonds

30 before purchasing it. But she went on feeling the soft, shiny, luxurious[5] things—holding them up with both hands to see them glisten[6] and to feel them glide through her fingers like snakes.

---

1. **fifteen dollars:** Fifteen dollars in the 1890s would be worth about $310 today.
2. **darning:** mending.
3. **gaunt** (gawnt): very thin.
4. **tiara** (tee EHR ah): small crownlike headdress.
5. **luxurious** (luhg ZHUR ee uhs): costly; expensive.
6. **glisten** (GLIHS uhn): shine or sparkle.

Two blotches[7] came suddenly into her pale cheeks. She asked the clerk, "Are there any eights-and-a-half?" In fact, there were more of that size than of any other. There were pairs in light blue, lavender, black, and various shades of tan and gray. Mrs. Sommers selected a black pair and pretended to examine their texture, which the clerk assured her was excellent. "Well, I'll take this pair," she said, handing the girl a five-dollar bill and waiting for her change and her package. What a very small package it was! It seemed lost in the depths of her shabby old shopping bag.

Mrs. Sommers did not head for the bargain counter. She took the elevator to the ladies' waiting rooms and put on her new silk stockings. She felt freed from responsibility. How good was the touch of the raw silk on her flesh! She felt like lying back in the cushioned chair and enjoying the luxury of it. She did for a little while before putting her shoes on and tucking the cotton stockings into her bag. Then she headed to the shoe department and took her seat to be fitted. The clerk noticed that her old shoes were not as nice as her stockings.

Mrs. Sommers held back her skirts and turned her feet one way and her head another as she glanced down at the polished, pointed-tipped boots. Her foot and ankle looked so very pretty that she could not believe they belonged to her. She wanted an excellent and stylish fit, she told the clerk—even if it cost a dollar or two more.

She had not been fitted with gloves in a long time. What gloves she did buy were always "bargains," so cheap that it would have been silly to expect them to be fitted to the hand. Now she rested her elbow on the cushion of the glove counter, and a pretty young woman drew a long kid[8] glove over Mrs. Sommers's hand, smoothing the glove and buttoning it neatly. Both women lost themselves in admiring the little gloved hand. But there were other places to spend money.

At a bookstall, Mrs. Sommers bought high-priced magazines such as she had been used to reading in the days when she had been used to other pleasant things. Her stockings, boots, and fitted

7. **blotches** (BLAHCH uhs): large spots of color.
8. **kid:** the skin of a young goat.

A PAIR OF SILK STOCKINGS **141**

Your TURN

MOTIVATION

A writer seldom states a character's motivation directly. You have to infer it from clues in the text and what you already know about people. Why do you think Mrs. Sommers feels free from responsibility (line 44)? Write your answer on the lines below.

_____

_____

_____

_____

_____

Your TURN

ANALYZING HISTORICAL CONTEXT

In lines 51–64, underline examples of what women wore in Mrs. Sommers's day. How are her clothes different from or the same as those women wear today?

_____

_____

_____

_____

_____

_____

_____

gloves gave her assurance, a sense of belonging to the well-dressed crowd. She was very hungry. Usually she would have waited

70 till she was home to have a cup of tea and a snack of whatever was handy, but not today.

She had often glimpsed a nearby restaurant with spotless tablecloths, shining crystal, and fashionable people. She was glad no one looked at her with surprise as she entered. She told the

75 waiter she did not want a large meal, just a nice, tasty bite—a half-dozen oysters, a plump chop, ice cream, a glass of wine, and a small cup of black coffee.

Waiting to be served, she removed her gloves leisurely,[9] laid them beside her, and cut open the pages of a magazine with her

80 knife. The crystal was more sparkling and the tablecloth whiter than they had seemed through the window. Quiet ladies and gentlemen lunched at small tables like her own. Soft, pleasing music played; a gentle breeze blew through the window. She tasted a bite, sipped her wine, and wiggled her toes in the silk stockings. The price made no

85 difference.

She still had money when she spotted a matinée poster. When she entered the theater, the play had begun, and the house seemed packed. But there were vacant seats here and there, and she was ushered to one between brilliantly dressed women who

90 had gone there to kill time, eat candy, and display their gaudy[10] attire. There were many others who were there solely for the play and acting. It is safe to say there was no one present who had quite the attitude that Mrs. Sommers did toward her surroundings. She gathered in the whole—stage, players, and people—in one wide

95 impression and absorbed and enjoyed it. She laughed at the comedy and wept—she and the gaudy woman next to her wept over the tragedy. And they talked a little together over it, and the gaudy woman wiped her eyes and sniffled on a tiny square of filmy, perfumed lace and passed little Mrs. Sommers her box of candy.

---

9. **leisurely** (LEEZH uhr lee): without hurry.
10. **gaudy** (GAWD ee): too showy.

100 The play was over, the music stopped; the crowd filed out. It was like a dream ended. People scattered in all directions. Mrs. Sommers went to the corner and waited for the cable car.

A man with sharp eyes, who sat opposite her, seemed to like looking at her small, pale face. He studied what he saw there. In
105 truth, he saw nothing—unless he could detect a touching wish, a powerful longing that the cable car would never stop anywhere, but go on and on with her forever.

Your
TURN

MOTIVATION

Re-read the last paragraph. Why do you think Mrs. Sommers would want the cable car to go on and on forever?

_____

_____

_____

_____

_____

_____

_____

_____

Motivation Chart

You already know a lot about **motivation**—the reasons for people's behavior—from your own experience and from observing other people. Use that knowledge as well as details in the short story to fill in the chart below. In the left-hand column are quotes from "A Pair of Silk Stockings." In the right-hand column, describe what you think the motivation is for Mrs. Sommers's behavior. One has been done for you.

Quote from the Story	Motivation
1. "The vision of her children looking fresh and dainty and new for once in their lives excited her." (lines 12–13)	
2. "She herself had no time—not one second to think about the past." (lines 16–17)	Mrs. Sommers was too busy taking care of her family to think about how her life used to be different.
3. "She wanted an excellent and stylish fit, she told the clerk—even if it cost a dollar or two more." (lines 54–56)	
4. "She was glad no one looked at her with surprise as she entered." (lines 73–74)	
5. "She gathered in the whole—stage, players, and people—in one wide impression and absorbed and enjoyed it." (lines 94–95)	

Vocabulary Development

Synonyms and Antonyms

For each of the vocabulary words below, write a synonym and an antonym in the space provided. Remember, a synonym is a word that has the same or almost the same meaning as another word—for example, *dawn* and *daybreak.* An antonym is a word that has the opposite meaning of another word—for example, *light* and *dark.* The first word has been done for you.

| **Synonym** | **Vocabulary Word** | **Antonym** |

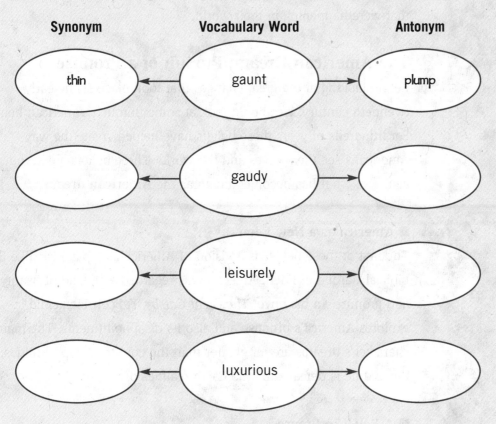

The Moderns: 1914–1939
Based on the Student Edition text
by John Leggett and John Malcolm Brinnin

Here's HOW

VOCABULARY

The word *voice* (line 1) is kind of confusing. Usually it refers to the sounds people make, like *The coach has a loud voice* or *The singer has a beautiful voice.* But what kind of voice does fiction have? The dictionary tells me that *voice* is "the writer's or speaker's distinctive use of language in a text." That makes sense here.

World War I (1914–1918) changed the United States and the voice of its fiction. The war seemed to take away the nation's innocence. Americans began to question their old values and beliefs. The traditions of the past were fading. In the arts the **modernist**
5 movement reflected these changes. Writers, painters, and musicians were no longer interested in or excited by traditional ways of making art. They called for bold, new styles that could express the changes that were happening in their world.

The American Dream: Pursuit of a Promise

10 Before looking at the great changes that took place in the early twentieth century, we should look at some uniquely American beliefs. For hundreds of years these beliefs have helped create the way Americans see themselves and the world. Three beliefs are at the center of what has become known as the **American dream.**

15 ■ **America as a New Eden**
The first of these beliefs is a vision of America as a paradise, like the biblical Garden of Eden. America was regarded as a land of beauty and promise. In his novel *The Great Gatsby,* F. Scott Fitzgerald explores America's promise and also its disappointments. The main
20 character's dreams are far greater than the country's opportunities. In the end he is defeated by the harsh realities of modern life.

■ **A Belief in Progress**
The second belief is optimism. America has long been seen as a place where dreams come true. As a young country the United States
25 offered what seemed like unlimited opportunity and wealth. Americans had come to believe in progress. They thought that life would keep getting better and that a perfect world could be made.

■ Triumph of the Individual

The third belief is in the importance of the individual. Nothing is out
30 of reach for an independent, confident person. An early writer who
helped define the American dream was Ralph Waldo Emerson. He
wrote that if a person trusts the universe and trusts himself, "the huge
world will come round to him."

A Crack in the World: Breakdown of Beliefs
35 and Traditions

World War I and the Great Depression hurt belief in the American
dream. Writers began to reject the values that had been handed down
from the Puritans in New England. The literary center of the nation
changed. Writers in the nineteenth century had been born in New
40 England. After the war, however, many new, different American
writers came instead from the South, the Midwest, and the West.

   In the postwar period two new trends in thought helped further
weaken traditional beliefs and values: **Marxism** and **psychoanalysis.**

Marxism and the Challenge to Free Enterprise

45 The first trend, Marxism, grew out of the writings of Karl Marx
(1818–1883). His beliefs in communal ownership and production had
fueled a revolution in Russia during World War I. These beliefs were
opposite to the American beliefs in private ownership and production.
Some Americans thought that Marxism could bring much-needed
50 rights to workers. However, other people worried that these new ideas
could spark a revolution in America too.

Freud and the Unconscious Mind

Sigmund Freud (1856–1939) developed psychoanalysis, the second
trend. Freud claimed that the unconscious mind controlled much
55 of human behavior. Americans were interested in this new field of
psychology. However, they also worried about the effect Freud's
theories might have on individual freedom. If our actions are really
controlled by our unconscious mind, how can we have free will?

Here's
HOW

VOCABULARY

I don't get how an unconscious
mind (line 54) can control
anything. I thought if you were
unconscious, you were asleep
or in a coma. Oh, I get it. Your
unconscious mind is the part
that dreams or that makes you
talk or walk in your sleep. It's
the part you can't control but
that sometimes controls things
you do.

Interest in the unconscious mind inspired a new literary style.
60 Writers used **stream of consciousness** to show the moment-by-moment flow of their characters' thoughts. The Irish writer James Joyce (1882–1941) used this style in his novel *Ulysses* (1922), and soon afterward American writers Katherine Anne Porter and William Faulkner followed.

65 ## At Home and Abroad: The Jazz Age

In 1919, Prohibition made it illegal to make or sell alcohol. The law was meant to get rid of what some thought of as a major social evil. Instead, Prohibition gave birth to an era of bootleggers,[1] gangsters, flappers,[2] and jazz. F. Scott Fitzgerald gave this energetic and intense
70 era in American history its name: the Jazz Age.

In 1920, women won the right to vote and became a presence in artistic, intellectual, and social circles. Despite the excitement of the Roaring Twenties in the United States, many writers and artists sought pleasure abroad. After World War I, living in France was both cheap
75 and exotic. To some people, life seemed better there, more luxurious. That so many Americans chose to live abroad was yet another sign that something had gone wrong with the American dream.

Grace Under Pressure: The New American Hero

Ernest Hemingway was a very influential post–World War I writer.
80 He sought to express bare truths as plainly and in as few words as possible. Hemingway also introduced a new kind of hero: disillusioned but also honorable and courageous. Hemingway fought his lack of faith with a belief in the self and in qualities such as decency, bravery, and skillfullness. He also believed that good, rich moments are rare
85 and that people should grab them before they get away.

Modern Voices in Poetry: A Dazzling Period of Experimentation

By the 1920s, American poetry had its own voice. It was no longer influenced by British poetry. The modernist artists Henri Matisse and
90 Pablo Picasso inspired many American poets who had moved to

---

1. **bootleggers** (BOOT LEHG uhrz): people who make illegal alcohol.
2. **flappers:** young women in the 1920s who broke social-conduct guidelines.

VOCABULARY

Underline the words that explain the technique of stream of consciousness (lines 60–61).

VOCABULARY

You probably know the root word in *prohibition* (line 66). There is also a good context clue in the following words. Use your prior knowledge and the context clue to figure out the meaning of *prohibition*, and write the definition on the lines below. Use a dictionary if you are having trouble.

_____

_____

_____

VOCABULARY

Maybe I can figure out what *disillusioned* (line 81) means by breaking it into parts. The prefix *dis–* means "away or apart," and an *illusion* is a "false idea," so *disillusioned* has something to do with getting away from false ideas. If that's so, why is there a *but* in the sentence? I better look it up. The dictionary says *disillusion* means "to take away ideals and cause disappointment or bitterness." Now the *but* makes sense.

Europe. Like these painters, the poets began looking at new ways of thinking and seeing the world. Ezra Pound and T. S. Eliot were part of an artistic trend called **symbolism.** Symbolists believed that striking images were more powerful than direct statements of feeling. Pound

95 also helped begin a related movement called **imagism.** Imagists such as E. E. Cummings presented hard, clear images in everyday words.

Voices of American Character

Some American poets rejected modernism. They stayed in the United States instead of travelling to Europe for inspiration. These poets

100 preferred to write in plain American speech. Their writings reflected the diverse spirit of the different American regions in which they lived and wrote.

The greatest of these poets was Robert Frost (1874–1963). He skillfully used ordinary New England speech in his writing. In a time

105 when "good" meant "new," Frost was unique in creating his own voice using traditional poetic forms.

The Harlem Renaissance: Voices of the African American Experience

During this time a group of African American poets drew heavily from

110 their own culture. They wrote poems that echoed the rhythms of jazz music. Their lyrics were like blues songs, and their language was from the poor city neighborhoods in which many African Americans lived.

James Weldon Johnson, Claude McKay, Countee Cullen, and Langston Hughes led this literary movement. It was part of a larger

115 artistic movement known as the **Harlem Renaissance,** because it was centered in the New York City neighborhood Harlem. African Americans had long been ignored in American art, but now they would be heard.

The American Dream Revised

120 The writers of the modernist era experimented with bold ways of writing. They tried writing about new subjects. But like those writers who came before and after them, they still asked the basic human questions: *Who are we? Where are we going? What values will guide us there?*

Winter Dreams

Literary Focus: Motivation

Do you ever wonder why a character does something? If so, you are thinking about the character's motivation. **Motivation** is the reason for a character's behavior. Sometimes a writer reveals motivation directly, by saying why the character does something. Other times you must figure out why the characters act as they do.

Reading Skill: Making Inferences About Character

Readers often use their prior experiences and knowledge to make **inferences,** or educated guesses, about what is happening in a text. When you read, you probably make inferences about why characters act as they do. For example, if you read that a character is crying, you might infer that something sad is happening in the character's life. Then you continue reading to gather other information to see if your inference is correct. You might want to record your inferences in a chart like the following one:

Inference Chart

Information	My Inference	True/False

Into the Story

This story is one of several that F. Scott Fitzgerald wrote about the dreams and illusions of the 1920s, the Jazz Age. "Winter Dreams" is about the pursuit of illusions and the unhappiness that follows. The story opens when fourteen-year-old Dexter is caddying, or carrying golf clubs, for wealthy golfers. He sees the girl of his dreams for the first time. The story spans eighteen years of Dexter's life.

Winter Dreams

BASED ON THE SHORT STORY BY
F. Scott Fitzgerald

Your
TURN

MOTIVATION

The story has given two reasons for Dexter quitting his caddie job: Judy Jones (line 16) and his "winter dreams" (line 26). Dexter's winter dreams are described in lines 5–9. On the lines below, explain how both reasons could be part of Dexter's motivation.

_____

_____

_____

_____

_____

_____

_____

Some of the caddies[1] were poor and lived in one-room houses with a skinny cow in the front yard, but Dexter Green's father owned the second-best grocery store in Black Bear, and Dexter caddied only for pocket money.

5   In snow season, Dexter dreamed of the summer and imagined himself a golf champion—sometimes he won easily, sometimes he came from behind. Sometimes he stepped from a sports car; or, surrounded by an admiring crowd, he demonstrated fancy diving in the club pool. Among those who watched open-mouthed was Mr.

10 Mortimer Jones. One day, Mr. Jones—himself and not his ghost—said, with tears in his eyes, that Dexter was the best caddy in the club. Jones wanted Dexter to continue to caddy for him.

But Dexter said, "No, sir, I'm fourteen; I'm too old to caddy."

"The best caddy I ever saw," shouted Mr. Mortimer Jones.

15 "Never lost a ball! Willing! Intelligent! Quiet! Honest! Grateful!"

Mr. Jones's daughter was the reason Dexter quit. Judy Jones was eleven and promised to be thoroughly lovely in a few years. She appeared on the course at nine o'clock one morning, her smile radiant, convincing.

20 Dexter watched her. Suddenly, he laughed and began to hurry away.

Miss Jones called him back and asked him to caddy. Dexter said, "I think I'll quit." His decision frightened him. He was a favorite caddy, and the thirty dollars a month he earned was more than he

25 could get elsewhere. But, as so often would be the case in the future, Dexter was ruled by his winter dreams.

II

These winter dreams later persuaded Dexter to choose a famous Eastern university—where he was the poor boy—over a more affordable state one. He wanted not just to see glittering things but

30 to have them himself.

---

1. **caddies:** people who assist golfers, carrying the clubs, finding balls, and so on.

After college he went to a city near Black Bear Lake. He made money. While rich men's sons peddled bonds,[2] Dexter borrowed a thousand dollars on his college degree and bought a partnership in a small laundry. Before he was twenty-seven, he owned the largest
35 string of laundries in his area.

But back when he was twenty-three, he went to Sherry Island Golf Club where he met Judy Jones again when her golf ball hit one of his golfing partners.

That evening Dexter swam to a raft on the lake. Over on a dark
40 peninsula, a piano was playing a tune from his college days. The tune made him feel that he was in step with life and that everything around him was radiating a glamour he might never know again.

In the darkness he heard a racing motorboat. Suddenly the boat was beside him, drowning out the hot tinkle of the piano. A
45 voice called out, "Who's that?" Then, as she reached the raft, "Weren't you on the golf course?"

He was.

"If you can drive a boat, you could drive this one so I can ride on the surfboard behind. I'm Judy Jones, and there is a man waiting
50 at my house for me. When he drove up, I drove out of the dock because he says I'm his ideal."

After being hauled by the boat for a while, she shouted, "What's your name?"

He told her.

55 "Well, why don't you come to dinner tomorrow night?"

For the second time, her casual whim[3] changed his life.

III

Waiting for her the next evening, Dexter imagined the men who had already loved Judy Jones—prep-school types who wore graceful clothes and had deep tans. Dexter now wore clothes from the best
60 tailors in America. He knew that dressing carelessly required more

---

2. **peddled bonds:** sold stocks and bonds in the financial market to wealthy investors.
3. **whim:** a sudden desire.

Here's HOW

MAKING INFERENCES

Dexter built his business from one laundry to a whole string of them before he was twenty-seven (lines 32–35)! I'd say he has a lot of initiative. I guess he wants to make a lot of money so he can have glittering things (lines 29–30).

Your TURN

MAKING INFERENCES

In lines 49–53, we learn that Judy drove away from a man who admires her. She introduces herself but doesn't ask Dexter's name until he has done her a favor. What can you infer about Judy's character at this point? Write your inference on the lines below.

_____

_____

_____

_____

_____

confidence than dressing carefully did. But carelessness was for his children. His mother, an immigrant, came from the peasant class and spoke broken English. Her son must keep to the set patterns.

That evening he and Judy talked of his university, which she visited frequently, and of the city where he worked and where he would return to his prospering laundries. Then, after dinner, she led him onto the dark sun-porch and changed the mood. "Do you mind if I weep a little?" she said.

"I'm afraid I'm boring you," he responded.

"No, I like you, but I've just had a terrible afternoon. A man I cared about said that he was as poor as a church mouse. He'd never even hinted it before."

"Perhaps he was afraid to tell you."

"Probably," she answered. "He didn't start right. Well, I've been mad about loads of poor men and fully intended to marry them all. But I hadn't thought of him that way, and my interest in him wasn't strong enough to survive the shock. Let's start right," she interrupted herself. "Are you poor?"

"No," he said frankly, "I'm probably making more money than any other man my age in the Northwest."

She smiled. A lump rose in Dexter's throat. She showered him with kisses that were not a promise but a fulfillment. It did not take him many hours to decide that he had wanted Judy Jones ever since he was a little boy.

IV

It began like that—and continued, with varying shades of intensity right up to the denouement.

With her head against his shoulder that first night, Judy whispered, "Last night I thought I was in love with a man, and tonight I think I'm in love with you." It seemed to him a beautiful, romantic thing to say. But a week later she took him to a picnic supper and later disappeared with another man. When she assured Dexter that she had not kissed the other man, he knew she was

lying—yet he was glad that she took the trouble to lie to him. He was one of a varying dozen who courted her. Each of them had at
95 one time been the favorite. When a new man came to town, dates were automatically canceled.

Getting what she wanted and using her charms amused Judy Jones. At first she and Dexter seemed to share a deep mutual attraction. That first August, they enjoyed three days of long
100 evenings on her dusky veranda,[4] of late afternoon kisses behind protecting garden trellises,[5] of mornings when she was fresh as a dream and almost shy in the daylight. There was all the ecstasy of an engagement about it, enhanced by the fact that there was no engagement. During that time, he had asked her to marry him. She
105 said, "Maybe some day." She said, "Kiss me." She said, "I'd like to marry you." She said, "I love you." Then she said nothing.

The three days were interrupted by the arrival of a New York man who visited at her house for half of September. To Dexter's agony, rumors said that they were engaged. But at the end of a
110 month, Judy was yawning. She told a local beau[6] that she was bored with her visitor, who left two days later looking very sad indeed.

On this note the summer ended. Dexter was twenty-four and could do as he wished. He went to dances where Judy Jones might
115 appear. He was an available young man and could have gone out socially as much as he liked. Already he was playing with the idea of going East to New York and taking Judy Jones with him. No reality could make her anything but desirable to him.

Summer, fall, winter, spring, another summer, another fall he
120 had given to Judy Jones. She had treated him with interest, with encouragement, with spite, with indifference, with contempt.[7] She had beckoned[8] him and yawned at him. She had brought him extreme happiness and unbearable pain. By autumn's end he realized he could not have Judy Jones.

---

4. **veranda** (vuh RAN duh): a long, open porch, usually with a roof.
5. **trellises** (TREH luhs iz): frames for climbing vines.
6. **beau** (boh): boyfriend.
7. **contempt:** scorn; lack of respect.
8. **beckoned:** motioned to come.

Here's HOW

MOTIVATION

Why does Dexter stay with Judy? She's running around with other men and lying to him. She must be awfully beautiful and exciting for him to put up with all that.

Here's HOW

MOTIVATION

In lines 105-106, Judy first says, "I'd like to marry you. I love you," but she doesn't say for sure that she will marry him. I think her motivation is to get a guy to fall in love with her and then keep him dangling! She must enjoy showing off her power!

Your TURN

MOTIVATION

Dexter is still motivated by his winter dreams, or fantasies. Underline the words in lines 113–118 that show Dexter doesn't face facts.

Your
TURN

MAKING INFERENCES

Re-read lines 125–130. What
can you infer about Dexter's
character? Underline the clues
that help you. Then, write your
inference on the lines below.

_____

_____

_____

_____

_____

_____

_____

Your
TURN

MOTIVATION

In lines 145–155, why do you
think Judy Jones tries to get
Dexter back?

_____

_____

_____

_____

_____

_____

_____

125   After a week of misery and hard work, Dexter went to a dance,
where he saw Judy with another man. He stayed late at the dance. He
sat for an hour with Irene Scheerer and talked about books and
music. He knew very little about either. But he thought the young and
already fabulously successful Dexter Green should know more about

130 such things.

That was in October, when he was twenty-five. In January,
Dexter and Irene became engaged. The engagement was to be
announced in June, and they were to be married three months later.

For the first time in over a year, Dexter was peaceful. Judy

135 Jones had been in Florida and afterward in Hot Springs, and
somewhere she had been engaged, and somewhere she had
broken it off. In the middle of May, a week before the planned
announcement of their engagement, Irene got sick and could not
attend a dance. Dexter went alone. He leaned against the door

140 post, nodded at a man or two—yawned.

"Hello, darling." The familiar voice at his elbow startled him.
Judy Jones had left a man and crossed the room to him. She was a
slender enameled[9] doll in cloth of gold.

He wondered if she knew of Irene Scheerer.

145   "You're handsomer than you used to be," she said thoughtfully.
"I'm awfully tired of everything, darling." She called everyone darling.
"I wish you'd marry me. I like the way you love me. Oh, Dexter, have
you forgotten last year?"

"No, I haven't forgotten."

150   Later, at her door, Judy said, "I hear you're giving Irene
Scheerer a violent rush."[10] Then Judy began to cry quietly. "I'm
more beautiful than anybody else. Why can't I be happy? I'd like to
marry you, if you'll have me, Dexter. I suppose you think I'm not
worth having, but I'll be so beautiful for you, Dexter." She added,

155 "Won't you come in?"

He heard her draw in her breath sharply. Waiting. "All right," his
voice was trembling, "I'll come in."

---

9. enameled: glossy, painted.
10. a violent rush: sudden, intense attention.

V

When the romance ended and even ten years later, he did not regret that night. The fact that Judy's interest endured just one
160 month seemed unimportant. The serious hurt he gave to Irene did not matter. Nor was he angry with Judy Jones. He loved her, and he would love her until the day he was too old for loving.

He went East in February, intending to settle in New York, but the war came to America[11] in March and changed his plans. He
165 went into the first officers' training-camp in late April. He was one of thousands of young men who greeted the war with relief, welcoming the freedom from tangled emotion.

VI

Seven years later, when he was thirty-two years old, in New York, where he had done well, a man named Devlin from Detroit came to
170 see him on business.

"You're from the Middle West," said Devlin. "The wife of one of my best friends came from your city. Judy Simms. Judy Jones she was once."

"Yes, I knew her," Dexter said. He had heard that she was
175 married.

"Lud Simms drinks and runs around. Judy's a little old for him."

"Why, she's only twenty-seven," cried Dexter.

Devlin continued, "She always forgives him. I think she loves him. They won't divorce." He added, "She was a pretty girl when
180 she first came to Detroit."

"Judy Jones was not a pretty girl. She was a great beauty," Dexter exclaimed.

Devlin laughed pleasantly. "She's a nice girl. I like her. I can't understand how a man like Lud Simms could fall madly in love with
185 her, but he did. Perhaps I've forgotten how pretty she was at her wedding. She has nice eyes."

---

11. **"the war came to America":** a reference to World War I.

Your TURN

MAKING INFERENCES

Lines 165–167 state that going to war was a relief for Dexter. What do you think Dexter is escaping?

_____

_____

_____

_____

_____

Your TURN

MAKING INFERENCES

What do you think happened to Judy Jones after she got married that made her change from a woman who carelessly hurt others to someone who is hurt herself?

_____

_____

_____

_____

_____

_____

_____

_____

What is the thing that "will come back no more" that Dexter refers to in lines 193–194?

_____

_____

_____

_____

_____

_____

_____

Dexter knew that he had just lost something, as surely as if he had married Judy Jones and seen her fade away before his eyes. The dream was gone. Even the grief he could have lived with was left

190 behind in the country of illusion, of youth, of the richness of life, where his winter dreams had thrived.

"Long ago," he said, "long ago, there was something in me, but now it is gone. I cannot cry. I cannot care. That thing will come back no more."

Making Inferences

An **inference** is a type of guess. To make an inference, you read carefully. Then you apply what you know to make a guess. Use the chart below to practice making inferences. First, read the quotation in the box on the left-hand side of the chart. Think about what it tells you about the character. (You may want to go back to the story and read some of the sentences around the quotation.) Then, in the box on the right-hand side of the chart, write what you infer from the quotation. The first one has been done for you.

Quotation	Your Inference . . .
1. "Dexter dreamed of the summer and imagined himself a golf champion—sometimes he won easily, sometimes he came from behind." (lines 5–7)	about Dexter: Dexter's dreams are more ambitious than his current life as a middle-class boy who caddies for spending money.
2. "'There is a man waiting at my house for me. When he drove up, I drove out of the dock because he says I'm his ideal.'" (lines 49–51)	about Judy:
3. "Already he was playing with the idea of going East to New York and taking Judy Jones with him." (lines 116–117)	about Dexter:
4. "'I'm more beautiful than anybody else. Why can't I be happy? I'd like to marry you, if you'll have me, Dexter.'" (lines 151–153)	about Judy:
5. "'She's a nice girl. I like her. I can't understand how a man like Lud Simms could fall madly in love with her, but he did. Perhaps I've forgotten how pretty she was at her wedding.'" (lines 183–186)	about Judy:

A Rose for Emily

Literary Focus: Setting

The **setting** of a story is its time and place. The setting also includes the customs of the people at the time and place the story occurs. For instance, in a realistic story about the Pilgrims landing at Plymouth Rock in 1620, you wouldn't expect them to ride from their ship to land in a motorboat or listen to their radios for the latest news. Instead, they would row ashore and be out of touch with the rest of the world for months at a time.

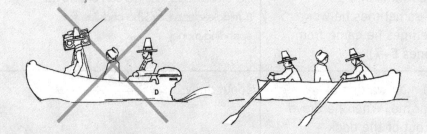

Reading Skill: Making Inferences About Character

Miss Emily surprises the townspeople with her strange behavior. As you read the story, take notes on her character. Include your ideas about the motivation, or reasons, for her actions.

Into the Short Story

This story takes place in Jefferson, Mississippi, at the turn of the twentieth century. As the story of Miss Emily unfolds, you will learn some important truths about the rest of her community—its loyalty to family and the past, its pride, its faithfulness to old values, its fierce independence, its scorn for the new, and its acceptance of segregation.

A Rose for Emily

BASED ON THE SHORT STORY BY

William Faulkner

I

When Miss Emily Grierson died, our whole town went to her funeral. The men went out of a sort of affection for a fallen monument. The women went to see the inside of her house. No one but an old servant had seen it in at least ten years. It was a big house with balconies on what was once the best street in town. But like the street, the house was now in a state of decay.

Miss Emily had been a tradition, a duty, and a care. It began in 1894, after her father died. At that time, the mayor, Colonel Sartoris, eliminated her taxes (not that Miss Emily would have accepted charity). Colonel Sartoris made up a tale that Miss Emily's father had loaned money to the town, and this was the town's way of paying it back.

When the next generation came to power, they rejected this arrangement. On the first of the year, they mailed her a tax notice. But February came, and there was no reply.

A group of aldermen[1] went to see her. The old Negro servant let them into a dim, stale-smelling hall. The parlor was furnished in worn, leather-covered furniture.

They rose when she entered. She was a small, fat woman in black, leaning on a cane. She looked bloated, like a drowned body. She did not ask them to sit. She just stood in the door and listened.

When she spoke, her voice was dry and cold. "I have no taxes in Jefferson. Colonel Sartoris explained it to me."

"But there is nothing in our records. We must go by the—"

"See Colonel Sartoris. I have no taxes in Jefferson."

"But, Miss Emily—"the aldermen protested.

"See Colonel Sartoris," she repeated. (Colonel Sartoris had been dead almost ten years.) "Tobe!" The Negro appeared. "Show these gentlemen out."

II

So she sent them away, just as she had sent away their fathers thirty years before about the smell. That was two years after her father's death and a short time after her sweetheart deserted her.

---

1. **aldermen:** town officials.

"A Rose for Emily" adapted from *Collected Stories of William Faulkner*. Copyright © 1930 and renewed © 1958 by William Faulkner; copyright © 2003 by Jill Faulkner Summers. Retold by Holt, Rinehart and Winston. All rights reserved. Reproduced by permission of **Lee Caplin, Representative for Faulkner Literary Estate.**

After her father's death, she went out very little. After her sweetheart went away, people hardly saw her at all. The only sign of life about the place was the Negro coming and going.

35 "As if any man could keep a kitchen properly," the ladies said. So they were not surprised when the smell developed.

The Board of Aldermen had to deal with the smell. "It's simple," the youngest said. "Send her word to have her place cleaned up. Give her a certain time to do it in, and if she don't . . . ."

40 Judge Stevens said, "Will you accuse a lady of smelling bad?"

So the next night, after midnight, four men slunk around Miss Emily's house like burglars. They broke open the cellar door and sprinkled lime there. As they recrossed the lawn, they saw Miss Emily in the window. After a time the smell went away.

45 People in our town believed that the Griersons had thought they were better than everyone else. None of the young men were quite good enough for Miss Emily and such. When her father died, we learned that the house was all that was left to her. In a way, people were glad. Being left alone and poor, she had become a more

50 sympathetic figure.

The day after his death, all the ladies prepared to call at the house, as is our custom. Miss Emily met them at the door, dressed as usual and with no trace of grief on her face. She told them that her father was not dead. She did that for three days. Just as they were

55 about to resort to law and force, she broke down, and they buried her father quickly.

We did not say she was crazy then. We remembered all the young men her father had driven away. It was natural that with nothing left, she would cling to the one who had robbed her.

III

60 She was sick for a long time. When we saw her again, her hair was cut short, like a girl's.

The town had just arranged for paving the sidewalks, and in the summer after her father's death, they began the work. The construction company's foreman was a Yankee named Homer

65 Barron—a man with rough good looks. Whenever you heard a lot

Your TURN

SETTING

Underline details in lines 35–40 that tell you about the roles of men and women at the time and place of this story. Then, describe those roles on the lines below.

_____

_____

_____

_____

_____

_____

_____

Your TURN

MAKING INFERENCES ABOUT CHARACTER

Re-read lines 45–50. What can you infer about the character of the townspeople from these lines? Write your inferences on the lines below.

_____

_____

_____

_____

_____

_____

_____

MAKING INFERENCES ABOUT CHARACTER

We learn about Homer Barron's character in lines 63–67. Underline details about him in the text. Then, describe on the lines below the kind of man you think he is.

_____

_____

_____

_____

MAKING INFERENCES ABOUT CHARACTER

What do you think the incident of the arsenic (lines 74–84) says about Miss Emily's character? Describe your inferences on the lines below.

_____

_____

_____

_____

SETTING

You can learn about some customs of the time in lines 85–90. What do you learn about attitudes toward men and women dating?

_____

_____

_____

_____

of laughing anywhere about the square, Homer Barron would be in the center of the group. Soon we began to see him and Miss Emily on Sunday afternoons driving in a yellow-wheeled buggy.

The ladies all said, "Of course a Grierson would not think
70 seriously of a Northerner, a day laborer." But eventually the old people began saying, "Poor Emily."

She carried her head high—even when we thought she was fallen. It was as if, as the last Grierson, she demanded more respect than ever. For instance, there was the arsenic matter.

75 "I want some poison," she said to the druggist. She was over thirty then, still a slight woman, with cold, haughty black eyes. "I want some poison," she said.

"Yes, Miss Emily. What kind? For rats and such? I'd recom—"

"Arsenic," Miss Emily said. "Is that a good one?"

80 "Why, of course," the druggist said. "If that's what you want. But the law requires you to tell what you are going to use it for."

Miss Emily just stared at him, her head tilted back, until he looked away and went and got the arsenic. When she opened the package at home, she saw "For rats" had been written on the box.

IV

85 So the next day we all said, "She will kill herself"; and we said it would be the best thing. It seemed as if Homer Barron would never marry her. We began saying, "Poor Emily," as they passed on Sunday in the buggy, Miss Emily with her head high and Homer Barron with his hat cocked and a cigar in his teeth. Some of the ladies said that it
90 was a disgrace.

Then, suddenly, we were sure that they were to be married. We learned that Miss Emily had purchased a man's hairbrush, comb, and mirror, with the letters H. B. on each piece. Two days later, we learned that she had bought an outfit of men's clothing, including a
95 nightshirt. We said, "They are married." We were really glad.

A neighbor saw the Negro man let Homer Barron in at the kitchen door one evening. That was the last we saw of Barron and of Miss Emily for some time. For almost six months she did not appear on the streets.

100   When we next saw Miss Emily, she had grown fat. During the next few years, her hair turned iron gray.

From that time on, her front door remained closed. Each December, we sent her a tax notice, which would be returned by the post office a week later, unclaimed. Thus, she passed from generation
105 to generation.

She died in one of the downstairs rooms, her gray head propped on a pillow moldy with age.

V

The Negro let the ladies in at the front door. He walked right through the house and out the back and was not seen again.

110   They held the funeral on the second day, with the town coming to look at Miss Emily beneath a mass of bought flowers. Already we knew that there was one room upstairs that no one had seen in forty years and which would have to be forced. They waited until Miss Emily was buried before they opened it.

115   The room was decked out as if for a bride, but dust lay everywhere: on the curtains, on the dressing table, on the man's brush and mirror. Upon a chair hung the suit, carefully folded; beneath it, the two shoes and the discarded socks.

The man himself lay in the bed.

120   For a long while we just stood there, staring. The body had apparently once lain in the position of an embrace. What was left of his rotting corpse had dissolved into the bed.

Then we noticed that in the second pillow was the indentation of a head. One of us lifted something from it. Leaning forward—the dust
125 dry and bitter in our nostrils—we saw a long strand of iron-gray hair.

Here's HOW

SETTING

I think it is unusual that someone could live in a small town for so long without seeing anyone. People in that town seem to have great respect for tradition and for privacy. They leave you alone to do what you want.

Your TURN

MAKING INFERENCES ABOUT CHARACTER

What do you think the long strand of iron-gray hair on the pillow (line 125) tells you about Miss Emily's character?

_____

_____

_____

_____

_____

_____

_____

_____

Setting Chart

The **setting** of a story is its time and place—as well as its customs. You can learn a lot about a story's setting from its details. Details from "A Rose for Emily" are listed in the left-hand column of the chart below. In the right-hand column, fill in what these details tell you about the setting. The first item has been done for you.

Quote from Story	What It Says About the Setting
1. "'Tobe!' The Negro appeared. 'Show these gentlemen out.'" (lines 28–29)	Miss Emily's servant is the only African American mentioned, so I'd say this is a segregated Southern town.
2. "The day after his death, all the ladies prepared to call at the house, as is our custom." (lines 51–52)	
3. "The ladies all said, 'Of course a Grierson would not think seriously of a Northerner, a day laborer.'" (lines 69–70)	
4. "Already we knew that there was one room upstairs that no one had seen in forty years and which would have to be forced. They waited until Miss Emily was buried before they opened it." (lines 111–114)	

Vocabulary Development

Multiple-Meaning Words

In English many words have more than one meaning. For each quote below, circle the letter of the following sentence in which the underlined word is used in the same way it is used in the quote. One has been done for you.

1. "Miss Emily had been a tradition, a duty, and a care."
   a. Take care that you don't get wet.
   b. He hadn't a care in the world.
   c. Don't you care about me at all?
   d. We care about the sick and the hungry.

2. "On the first of the year, they mailed her a tax notice."
   a. Did you notice the girl with blue hair?
   b. It is polite not to notice when someone burps.
   c. Her performance received a good notice in the paper.
   d. I received a notice that my library book was overdue.

3. "When she spoke, her voice was dry and cold."
   a. Brrrrr! It's cold outside!
   b. I can't play today. I've got a cold.
   c. He glared with cold, mean eyes.
   d. She had her lines for the play down cold.

4. "'As if any man could keep a kitchen properly,' the ladies said."
   a. You cannot keep that dirty dog in my clean house!
   b. Can't you ever keep your room clean?
   c. Keep this ring as a symbol of our friendship.
   d. The weapons were stored in the castle's keep.

5. "Whenever you heard a lot of laughing anywhere in the square, Homer Barron would be in the center of the group."
   a. How do you determine the area of a square?
   b. I love to go square dancing!
   c. He's boring; he likes such square music.
   d. The met for the first time in the town square.

Nobel Prize Acceptance Speech, 1950

Literary Focus: Public Speaking

Public speaking is the art of making a speech. Because speeches are written to be heard, the way a speech sounds is important. To make you remember what you hear, a speechwriter uses devices such as **parallelism, contrast,** and **repetition.**

```
                    ┌─────────────────────┐
                    │   Public Speaking   │
                    └─────────────────────┘
```

Parallelism	Contrast	Repetition
Using the same grammatical form to balance related ideas: *To live simply and to breathe fresh air— that's what I want.*	Putting contrasting ideas in a balanced construction: *Uncle Charlie frowned not in anger but in puzzlement.*	Repeating words to cause emotion, emphasize ideas, or clarify ideas: *If you win, we win. Working together, we all win.*

Reading Skill: Finding the Main Idea

The **main idea** is the central idea of the speech. To find the main idea, follow these steps:

- Identify the important details in the speech.
- Think about the point the important details make.
- From this information, figure out what the main idea is.

Into the Speech

William Faulkner accepted the Nobel Prize in literature in 1950, five years after the United States dropped nuclear bombs on Japan. By 1949, the Soviet Union had become the second nuclear power. At the time of this speech, many people were worried that there might be a worldwide nuclear war. Life had become very uncertain. In his speech, Faulkner urges young writers to avoid literature based on "physical fear." He urges them to focus on the eternal questions of "the human heart in conflict with itself."

Nobel Prize
Acceptance Speech, 195

BASED ON THE SPEECH BY
William Faulkner

I feel that this award was not made to me, but to my work. It will not be difficult to find a proper use for the money. To find a proper use for the acclaim, I want to use this moment to speak to young writers everywhere. They are dedicated to the hard effort of creative work, and one of them will stand here someday.

Our tragedy today is a universal physical fear. There are no longer problems of the spirit. There is only the question: When will I be blown up? This question has made young writers forget the problems of the human heart in conflict with itself, which is the only thing worth writing about, worth the agony and the sweat.

The young writer must teach himself that the basest thing of all is to be afraid; and, teaching himself that, he must forget it forever. He must leave no room in his mind for anything but the old truths of the heart. Any story without these old universal truths—love and honor and pity and pride and compassion and sacrifice—is doomed. Without these truths he writes not of love but of lust, of defeats in which nobody loses anything of value, and of victories without hope and, worst of all, without pity or compassion. He grieves for nothing that is truly important. He writes not of the heart but of the glands.

Until a writer relearns these things, he will write as though he watched the end of man. I refuse to accept the end of man. It is easy enough to say that man is immortal simply because he will endure: that when the last dingdong of doom has clanged and faded from the last dying evening, that there will still be one more sound—that of man's puny voice, still talking. I refuse to accept this. I believe that man will not merely endure: he will prevail. He is immortal because he has a soul, a spirit capable of sympathy, sacrifice, and endurance. The writer's duty is to write about these things. It is his privilege to help man endure by lifting his heart, by reminding him of the courage and honor and hope and pride and compassion and pity and sacrifice that have been the glory of his past. The writer's voice need not merely be the record of man. It can instead be one of the pillars that will help him endure and prevail.

Public Speaking

Public speaking is the art of making a speech. Speechwriters use a variety of techniques to make their words inspiring or persuasive. These techniques include parallelism, contrast, and repetition:

- **Parallelism** is using the same grammatical form to balance related ideas: *I will help by mowing the yard, cleaning the garage, and walking the dog.*

- **Contrast** is putting contrasting ideas in a balanced construction: *Mom cried not from sadness but from happiness.*

- **Repetition** is repeating words to clarify ideas, to emphasize ideas, or to cause emotion: *Step right up, ladies and gentlemen. Step right up to the greatest show on earth!*

In the chart below are excerpts from Faulkner's speech. Read each line from the speech in the left-hand column. Then, in the right-hand column, circle which technique is being used. Underline the words in the left-hand column that help you decide. One item has been done for you.

Lines from the Speech	Public-Speaking Technique
1. "I feel that this award was not made to me, but to my work." (line 1)	Parallelism Contrast Repetition
2. "the only thing worth writing about, worth the agony and the sweat" (lines 9–10)	Parallelism Contrast (Repetition)
3. "It is his privilege to help man endure by lifting his heart, by reminding him. . . ." (lines 28–29)	Parallelism Contrast Repetition

A Worn Path

Literary Focus: Theme

The **theme** of a story is its main idea or insight into life. A story's
theme is not the same as its subject, which can be stated in a
word or phrase such as *growing up, love, a special journey, heroism*
or *fear*. A story's theme is what the writer wants to say *about* the
subject. In "A Worn Path," Eudora Welty gives her point of view on
the journeys we take for those we love.

Reading Skill: Making Predictions

Part of the fun of reading is guessing what will happen. When you do
this, you are **making predictions.** To make a prediction, look for clues
in the text. As you get more information, you can keep revising your
predictions. If you guess right, you can congratulate yourself. If you
guess wrong, you can enjoy the surprise of what really does happen.

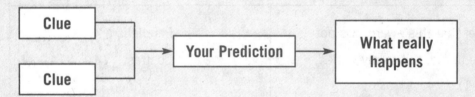

Into the Short Story

The sight of an old woman crossing a road in winter inspired
Eudora Welty to write "A Worn Path." Welty then invented the
errand that sent the woman on her journey and the people and
things she met along the way.

A Worn Path

BASED ON THE SHORT STORY BY

Eudora Welty

Here's HOW

THEME

The name of the woman in line 1 is Phoenix. I thought this was an unusual name, so I asked my teacher about it. He told me that a phoenix (FEE nihks) is a bird from mythology. It lives for 500 or 600 years and then burns itself and rises from its own ashes. This bird is often used in literature to represent dying and coming back to life. I'm going to pay attention to details in the story to see if the name Phoenix will help me understand the theme of the story.

Your TURN

THEME

Storytellers often use journeys to represent life. The difficulties that a main character faces along the journey often represent challenges a person has to deal with in life. Circle words or phrases in lines 9–25 that describe obstacles (difficulties) Phoenix faces.

On a cold December morning an old Negro woman named Phoenix Jackson walked slowly along a path through the woods. She carried a thin, small cane made from an umbrella, and with this cane she was tapping the frozen earth in front of her.

5   She wore a long dress and an apron made of old sugar sacks. Her shoelaces dragged behind her unlaced shoes. She looked straight ahead as she walked. Her eyes were blue with age, and her skin was wrinkled.

Now and then she heard noises in the thicket. "Out of my way,
10 all you wild animals!" Phoenix cried. She hit the bushes with her cane to scare them away. "I got a long way to go," she said.

As she walked, a thorn bush caught her dress. "I caught in the thorny bush," she said. "Thorns, you never want to let folks pass, no sir." Finally she managed to free herself.

15   When she came to the spot where a log lay across a rushing creek, Phoenix lifted her long skirt and closed her eyes. She stepped onto the log and marched across the creek. Safe on the other side, she said, "I wasn't as old as I thought."

She sat down to rest, trying hard not to close her eyes. When a
20 little boy brought her a piece of cake, she said, "That would be acceptable." When she reached for the cake, there was only air.

She came to a barbed-wire fence and crawled under it, careful not to let her dress be caught and torn. When she was clear of the fence, she looked up and saw a black buzzard in a tree. "Who you
25 watching?" she called out to the bird.

She entered a field of dead corn where there was no path and saw what looked like a man dancing ahead of her. At first she thought it was a ghost, but it turned out to be a scarecrow.[1]

A flock of little birds ran across her path. "Walk pretty," she
30 said. "This the easy place. This the easy going." She walked past old cabins, their doors and windows boarded up. At a spring, Phoenix bent to drink the clear, cold water. Then the path went through a swamp where she called out, "Sleep on, alligators."

---

1. **scarecrow** (SKAIR KROH): an image of a person that is supposed to scare away birds.

"A Worn Path" adapted from *A Curtain of Green and Other Stories* by Eudora Welty. Copyright 1941 and renewed © 1969 by Eudora Welty. Retold by Holt, Rinehart and Winston. Reproduced by permission of **Harcourt, Inc.**

Then there were trees that met overhead making the road as
35 dark as a cave. A black dog came out of the shadows and knocked
her into a ditch. "Old woman," she said to herself, "this dog come
along to slow you down. He's just sitting there on his fine tail, smiling
at you."

A young white hunter finally came along and said, "Well,
40 Granny, what are you doing there?" He lifted her up. "Anything
broken?" he asked.

"No, sir," said Phoenix. "I thank you for your trouble."

"Are you on your way home?" he asked.

"No, sir. Home is back that way. I'm going to town."

45 "Why, that's too far!" he said. "Now you go on home, Granny!"

"No sir," Phoenix said, "I have to go to town."

The man laughed at her, and she saw a shiny nickel drop from
his pocket.

"How old are you, Granny?" the man asked.

50 "There is no telling, mister," she said. "No telling."

"Well, I'd give you a dime," he said, "if I had any money with
me."

The man went away, and Phoenix gently lifted the shiny nickel
from the ground, putting it in her pocket. "God watching me the
55 whole time," she said. "Now I be stealing."

The man came back and pointed the gun at her. Phoenix
thought he was going to shoot her for stealing his nickel. But then
he smiled and put the gun down. "Get on home now," he said.

Phoenix finally came to the town, and there she asked a lady on
60 the street if she would tie Phoenix's shoes for her. "Untied shoes do
all right for out in the country," old Phoenix said, "but I need to go
into a big building." The woman told her to stand still and bent down
to tie the shoes.

Phoenix went into a big building and climbed many steps. Her
65 feet knew when to stop, and she went in a door. "Here I be," she
said.

Here's
HOW

MAKING PREDICTIONS

In lines 39–52, the hunter seems
like a nice guy because he picks
the old woman up after she has
fallen. But he also lies to her
about not having any money. He
may not be a bad guy, but I don't
trust him. Maybe something
strange is going to happen.

Here's
HOW

MAKING PREDICTIONS

Something strange did happen!
The hunter came back (line 56)
and pointed a gun at Phoenix.

Your
TURN

MAKING PREDICTIONS

You've already read two pages
of this story, and the writer
still hasn't explained why
Phoenix is making this trip.
Where do you think Phoenix
is going? Write your answer
below. Circle clues in the text
that helped you make your
prediction.

_____

_____

_____

_____

_____

_____

Eudora Welty Collection, Mississippi
Department of Archives and History.

Your TURN

MAKING PREDICTIONS

Underline words in lines 70–73 that explain why Phoenix made her trip. Then, compare this reason with the prediction you made with page 175. Why do you think the reason for Phoenix's journey was not revealed earlier? Write your answer below.

_____

_____

_____

_____

_____

_____

Your TURN

THEME

Phoenix plans to buy a windmill as a present for her grandson in lines 96–99. What other gift has Phoenix given him? How do these gifts contribute to the story's theme? Write your answer below.

_____

_____

_____

_____

_____

_____

"A charity case,[2] I suppose," said an attendant[3] sitting at a desk. "Speak up, Grandma, what's your name?" Phoenix did not speak. "Are you deaf?" cried the attendant.

70   A nurse came in and said, "That's just old Aunt Phoenix. She lives way back in the woods, and she comes to get medicine for her grandson. Have a seat, Aunt Phoenix. You look tired after your long walk."

The old woman sat straight in the chair. "Now, how is the boy?"
75 asked the nurse.

Old Phoenix was silent, her face solemn[4] and still.

The nurse became impatient. "I said, how is the boy? Is his throat any better?"

Finally the old woman spoke. "My grandson," she said. "It was
80 my memory had left me. I forgot why I made my long trip."

"Forgot?" said the nurse. "After you came so far?"

"My little grandson, he is still sick. I forgot," said Phoenix.

The nurse looked at some writing on a card. "He swallowed lye. Three years ago? He's not dead, is he?"

85   "No, missy," said Phoenix. "He's not dead. But he's very weak, and sometimes he can't swallow. He not able to help himself."

"All right," said the nurse, handing the old woman a bottle of medicine. "Charity," she said, making a check mark in a book.

Old Phoenix held the bottle close to her eyes, and then she put
90 it carefully in her pocket.

"I thank you," she said.

"It's Christmastime, Grandma," said the attendant. "Could I give you a few pennies out of my purse?"

"Five pennies is a nickel," said Phoenix.

95   "Here's a nickel," said the attendant.

Phoenix held her two nickels together in her hand. "This is what I'm going to do," she said. "I'm going to the store to buy a paper windmill for my grandson. I'll walk home holding it safe in my hand and give it to him."

100   She turned and walked out of the office and then slowly went down the stairs.

---

2. **charity case** (CHAR uh tee KAYS): a poor person who needs money and kindness.
3. **attendant** (uh TEHN duhnt): a servant or caretaker.
4. **solemn** (SAHL uhm): serious.

Theme

The **theme** of a story is its main idea. It is what the writer wants to say *about* the subject—the writer's special insight into life.

The theme of "A Worn Path" could be stated as "People find their way through all manner of obstacles, time after time, because of their love for someone." For each detail from "A Worn Path" shown below, write a sentence or two telling how the lines are especially important to this theme. Number 3 has been done for you.

Theme: People find their way through obstacles, time after time, because of their love for someone.

Details from Story	Relationship to Theme
1. The main character's name is Phoenix. (line 1)	**1.**
2. When the story opens, Phoenix is already walking along the path. (lines 1–2)	**2.**
3. The hunter points a gun at Phoenix, but she is not afraid. (line 56)	**3.** Phoenix's journey takes courage. She is completely devoted to her grandson. Her love makes her strong.
4. Phoenix plans to buy her grandson a paper windmill. (lines 97–98)	**4.**

Contemporary Literature: 1939 to Present

Based on the Student Edition text by John Leggett, Susan Allen Toth, John Malcolm Brinnin, and Thomas Hernacki

On August 6, 1945, the United States dropped an atomic bomb on the Japanese city of Hiroshima. Within seconds the center of the city had disappeared. The bomb ended World War II, but the memory of its giant mushroom cloud would linger in people's minds.

5   Many Americans disapproved of using the bomb. However, most supported the war itself as a struggle against tyranny. Twenty years later, though, the nation's involvement in the Vietnam War would divide its citizens. Feelings ran high, and demonstrations were common.

As the Vietnam war was winding down, Americans were again
10 disillusioned in 1974, when the Watergate scandal forced President Richard M. Nixon to resign.

In the 1980s, individual enjoyment and material success seemed to overshadow other concerns. Since the end of World War II, the United States and the Soviet Union had been locked in a bitter conflict
15 of words and politics, which involved no direct warfare, known as the cold war. Late in the decade the Soviet Union collapsed, ending the cold war. The threat of nuclear war was reduced but not destroyed.

In many ways the nuclear bomb is a symbol of the late twentieth century. Its terrifying mushroom cloud represents the triumph of
20 science and technology. The same science and technology that was meant to make life better had produced terrible results.

The Promise and Peril of Technology

In some ways, science and technology have made our lives better. We can live longer, travel faster, feed more people—and even walk
25 on the moon. However, many people still live in poverty. Computers have replaced many workers. The computer age has threatened the American ideal of the rugged individual. Many people feel that they have become faceless consumers who are known only by their

VOCABULARY

I don't hear people use the word *tyranny* (line 6) very often, but on the news they talk a lot about tyrants such as Saddam Hussein, Hitler, and Stalin. They were really bad guys who did terrible things to people, so I know I'm against tyranny.

VOCABULARY

Symbols (line 18) are people, animals, places, or things that have their own meaning but also stand for something else. What aspect of the late twentieth century does the symbol of the nuclear bomb's mushroom cloud represent?

_____

_____

_____

_____

_____

_____

computer password or their credit card number. They worry about
invasions of their privacy. They worry that mass advertising,
journalism, and entertainment may be shaping who they are and how
they see the world around them.

Contemporary Fiction: Diversity and Vitality

The term **postmodern** is often used to describe contemporary
American culture. In general, postmodernism is a departure from the
modernist art movement of the early twentieth century. Modernists,
such as Ezra Pound, T. S. Eliot, Katherine Anne Porter, and Ernest
Hemingway, used new styles and new forms to show how they saw
their world. Postmodern writers use many of the same tools, but the
works they produce are strikingly different.

■ Perspectives in Postmodern Fiction

Postmodern fiction goes beyond former limits. It can contain many
meanings and many worlds. Real worlds, dream worlds, and future
worlds may merge. Narrators and characters may tell different
versions of a story. A story may comment upon itself. It may also
allow for more than one interpretation. Postmodern fiction is known
for its sense of play, its range of cultural voices, and its blending of
fiction and nonfiction. It uses all the old tools in surprising new ways.

Characteristics of Postmodern Literature

- Allows for multiple meanings and worlds
- Is organized in nontraditional forms
- Comments upon itself
- Can be very personal
- Is culturally diverse
- Blends fiction and nonfiction
- Uses past forms and techniques in bold new ways

VOCABULARY

The word *postmodern* (line 34) is easy to figure out since I know that the prefix *post–* means "after." What I want to know, though, is what will come next. Will we have postpostmodern, or will they come up with a new name?

VOCABULARY

The word *play* as a noun can mean "a game or sport," "a drama," "fun," or "freedom of possibility." Which do you think it means in line 47?

_____

_____

Contemporary Nonfiction: Breaking the Barriers

Nonfiction works were long considered nonliterary too. People assumed that writing nonfiction required little artistic skill. Like
60 newspaper articles, nonfiction works were written and read quickly, then discarded. Critics focused on a search for the Great American Novel—the *true* literary art form.

Since the 1970s, though, nonfiction has gained popularity and respect. Books about computers, architecture, travel, film, and other
65 subjects are now taken seriously as art by critics and readers alike. Lists of bestsellers now often include memoirs, biographies, and histories.

■ Does It Have to Be Accurate?

This new popularity has come with several uncertainties, though.
70 Critics are unsure what terms they should use to discuss the art of nonfiction. In fiction we speak of elements such as point of view, character, plot, and setting. In more complex fiction we discuss irony, metaphors, symbols, and levels of meaning. However, these traditional terms don't always apply to nonfiction. In addition, nonfiction
75 presents the problem of accuracy. Readers expect a nonfiction work to be *true*. Yet a nonfiction work, such as an autobiography, might present a very slanted point of view.

■ The New Journalism

In the 1960s, the new journalism (also called literary journalism)
80 began to appear. New journalists used many of the elements of fiction. They also did not feel the need to keep personal material out of their writing. For example, Truman Capote became friends with the murderers he wrote about in his "nonfiction novel," *In Cold Blood*. Readers were as interested in the author's thoughts and feelings as
85 they were in the facts of the book.

Here's HOW

VOCABULARY

I don't really understand what a *nonfiction novel* (line 83) is. If it is nonfiction and true, how can it be a novel? I guess I'll have to read one to find out.

But if facts do not define nonfiction, what does? No one is sure. What readers *are* sure about is their interest in nonfiction that gives them compelling characters, suspense, and original insights.

Contemporary Poetry: Varied and Intensely Personal

90 In recent years more Americans have been writing poetry than ever before. It is difficult to determine which poets and movements will last.

■ The Decline of Modernism

American poetry is still evolving. However, there are a number of
95 clear differences between poetry today and the poetry that came before. The modernist poetry that thrived between World War I and World War II was largely defined by T. S. Eliot and Ezra Pound. Eliot called for a poetry that left out the poet's emotions. Pound insisted that the image was all-important and that any unnecessary words
100 should be left out.

By the 1950s, though, modernism no longer seemed appropriate. Post–World War II society craved the comfort of traditional values and material success. People still worried about the atomic bomb, but buying a house or a car seemed more important to daily life.

105 ### ■ The Beat Poets

In 1956, Allen Ginsberg published a long poetic outcry against the conformity of the 1950s. "I saw the best minds of my generation destroyed by madness, starving hysterical naked," *Howl* begins. The poem then continues in this way for hundreds of lines. Nothing could
110 be farther from the cool restraint of modernism.

Along with Jack Kerouac's novel *On the Road* (1957), *Howl* became a kind of bible for young nonconformists of the beat generation. The beat lifestyle of poetry readings, jazz, and late-night coffeehouses had a strong impact on American culture. The beat
115 poets were concerned about the injustices of modern life and the importance of imagination. These concerns would fuel the poetry of the 1960s.

Here's
HOW

VOCABULARY

I thought *hysterical* (line 108) meant "very funny," but that doesn't make sense in this quotation. I'd better look it up. The dictionary gives another definition that seems to fit here better: "wild and emotionally uncontrolled."

■ Poetry and Personal Experience

In 1959, Robert Lowell published a volume of verses called *Life*
120 *Studies*. These poems deal with life experiences such as alcoholism,
illness, and depression. These were personal subjects that the
modernists avoided. In doing so, Lowell helped to reunite T. S. Eliot's
"the man who suffers and the mind which creates."

When a critic described Lowell's poems as "confessional," the
125 name stuck. The **confessional school** of poets included Sylvia Plath,
Anne Sexton, and John Berryman. They wrote open, honest, and
sometimes brutal poems about their private lives.

■ History of the Human Heart

Since the 1970s, American poetry has become remarkably diverse.
130 The variety of styles and attitudes has attracted large new audiences.
Poetry performances have sprung up across America. Video and audio
technology, television, and the Internet have also helped poetry
become more available to the public.

Much contemporary American poetry echoes Walt Whitman by
135 celebrating the vast mix of people who call America home. Poetry
lives in the people, contemporary poets seem to say. Any walk of life,
any experience, can result in true poetry. These poets often write in
everyday language. They do not hesitate to surprise or even shock
with their language, attitudes, and private details.
140 The poet laureate, Billy Collins, suggests that contemporary
American poetry will survive because it is "the only history of the
human heart we have."

Where the Present Meets the Past on the Way to the Future

145 Every generation looks to their literature for a fresh voice and a new
attitude. Yet much contemporary American literature deals with the
themes of the past. The mark of true wisdom, Ralph Waldo Emerson
wrote, "is to find the miraculous in the common." However, it seems

Here's HOW

VOCABULARY

Line 140 has another word I don't know: *laureate*. I wonder if *laurel* is part of it. I remember from social studies that in ancient Rome a laurel wreath on the head was a sign of honor. A dictionary says I was right and that a *poet laureate* is a poet chosen as the official poet of a region. Since the sentence doesn't give a region, I'd guess Billy Collins is poet laureate of the United States.

more and more difficult to do so amidst the cheap clutter of modern
150 life. "I find myself . . . circling back to man's religious nature," the
novelist John Updike has written, "and the real loss to man and art
alike when that nature has nowhere to plug itself in." These words
might also describe the work of many contemporary writers.
The roots of these writers reach back to the nineteenth-century
155 Transcendentalists and even further back to those hardy Puritans
who crossed the Atlantic in their small wooden ships.

VOCABULARY

Do you remember what the
Transcendentalists (line 155)
believed? If not, look back at
pages 41–42. Then, write the
definition on the lines below:

_____

_____

_____

_____

_____

From The Way to Rainy Mountain

Literary Focus: Setting

Setting is the time and place of a story—when and where the story happens. Setting helps create the atmosphere, or mood, of a story.

A story doesn't have to take place in only one setting. Sometimes a writer moves the story from one place to another or tells us events that happened at an earlier time. These shifts or changes in setting can affect the mood of the story.

Reading Skill: Identifying Main Ideas and Supporting Details

Writers give us specific details to support their main ideas. These **supporting details** make the **main ideas** of a selection more interesting and more believable.

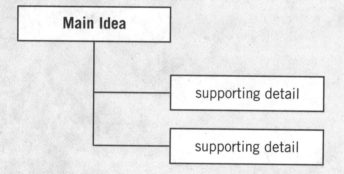

Into the Memoir

The Kiowas are Native Americans who once lived in the mountains of western Montana. In the middle of the seventeenth century, they moved onto the plains of present-day Oklahoma. In the mid–nineteenth century the Kiowas had to deal with another change—the arrival of European settlers.

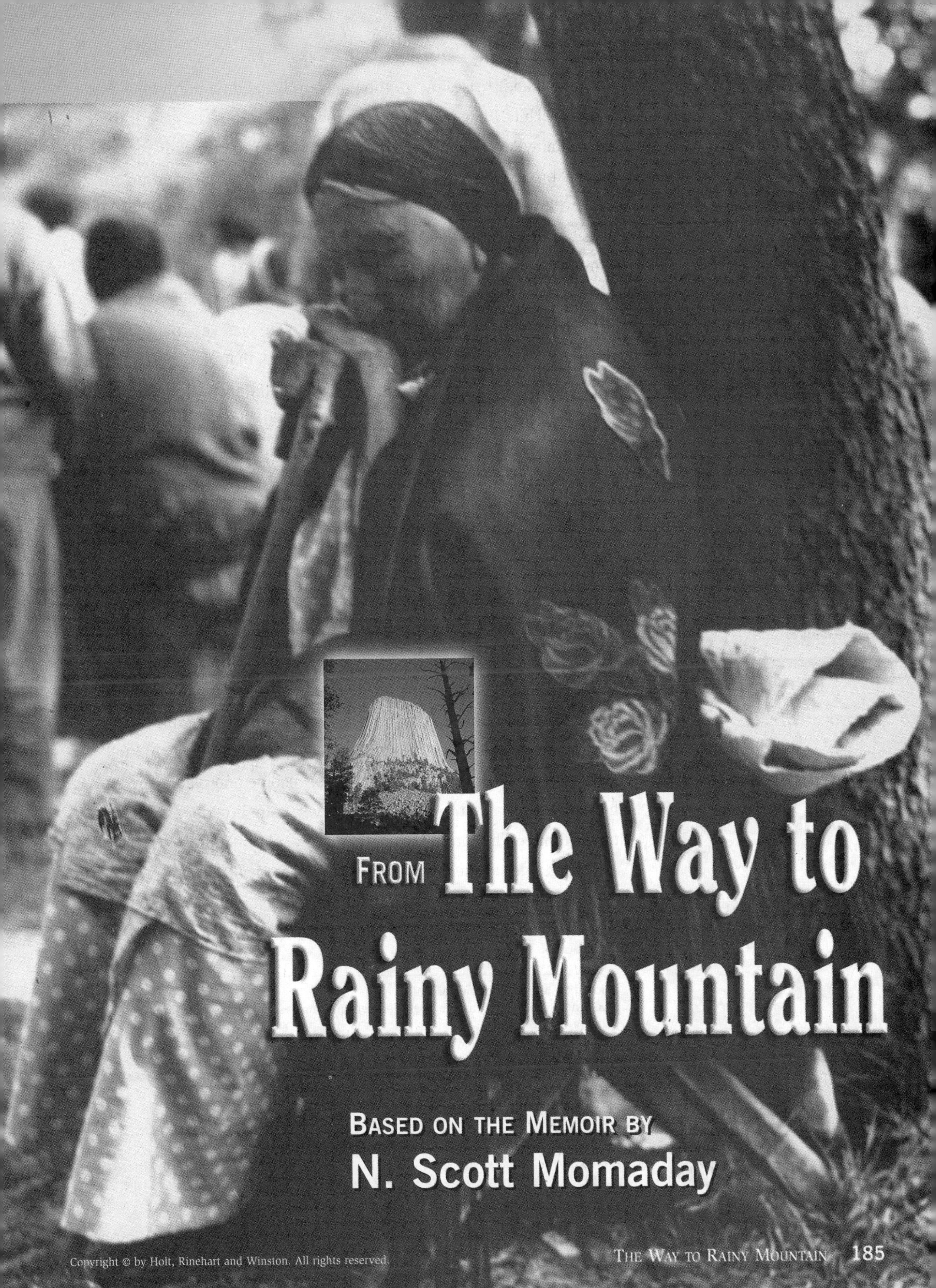

FROM **The Way to Rainy Mountain**

BASED ON THE MEMOIR BY

N. Scott Momaday

SETTING

Hard winters. Dry summers. A lonely land. It doesn't sound like my kind of place. I'm going to keep reading to find out why the writer finds this place special.

MAIN IDEAS AND SUPPORTING DETAILS

I'm supposed to look for main ideas and supporting details. OK, I'll start with the first paragraph. In line 3, the writer claims that Rainy Mountain has the "hardest weather in the world." That's his main idea. Then he gives examples to support that idea: blizzards in winter, extremely dry summers.

Your TURN

SETTING

The writer begins by describing Rainy Mountain in Oklahoma, but then he shifts to a different place. Circle the name of this other place in line 27. Why does the writer travel to this other place?

_____

_____

_____

_____

_____

_____

_____ .

A single knoll[1] rises out of the plains in Oklahoma north and west of the Wichita Range. Long ago my people, the Kiowas, gave it the name Rainy Mountain. The hardest weather in the world is there. Winter brings blizzards, but in the summer the prairie is brittle and
5 brown. It is a lonely land, and to look at that landscape is to lose the sense of proportion. Your imagination comes to life, and this, you think, is where Creation began.

I returned to Rainy Mountain in July to visit the grave of my grandmother, who had died in the spring. She was very old when she
10 died, but I was told that in death her face was that of a child.

When she was born, the Kiowas were living the last great moment of their history. For more than a hundred years, in alliance[2] with the Comanches, they had ruled the southern Plains.[3] They were warriors, but finally they were defeated by the U.S. Cavalry.

15 My grandmother's name was Aho. Her ancestors had come from the high country in western Montana nearly three hundred years ago. They were a mysterious tribe of hunters, mountain people with a language all their own. Over the years they journeyed toward the rising sun, slowly taking on the Plains culture and religion of the
20 Crows. The Kiowas acquired horses, took on the Sun Dance ritual, and shared the Crows' belief in the divinity of the sun.

Aho lived out her life in the shadow of Rainy Mountain, but the whole of the Plains was in her blood like a memory. She could tell stories of the Crows and the Black Hills,[4] people and places she had
25 never seen. I wanted to see for myself what she described, and so I traveled fifteen hundred miles to begin my pilgrimage.

When I got to the Black Hills, I could see Devils Tower.[5] There are things in nature that bring about an awesome quiet in the heart; Devils Tower is one of them.

---

1. **knoll** (nohl): a mound, a small hill.
2. **alliance** (uh LY uhns): a union between persons, families, or nations who share common interests.
3. **Plains, or Great Plains:** a semiarid region east of the Rocky Mountains in the United States and Canada.
4. **Black Hills:** mountains in southwest South Dakota and northeast Wyoming.
5. **Devils Tower:** a shaft of stone overlooking the Belle Fouche River in northeastern Wyoming.

From Introduction adapted from *The Way to Rainy Mountain* by N. Scott Momaday. Copyright © 1969 by **The University of New Mexico Press.** Retold by Holt, Rinehart and Winston. First published in *The Reporter*, January 26, 1967. Reproduced by permission of the publisher.

30   A Kiowa legend about the place tells about eight children, seven
sisters and their brother. One day, when they were playing, the
brother turned into a bear and began to chase the girls. They ran from
him, finding safety as they climbed onto the stump of a great tree that
began to rise into the air. The bear's claws scraped out grooves in the
35 bark of the tree, but the girls were out of reach. They escaped into the
sky to become the stars of the Big Dipper.

    From that moment, and so long as the legend lives, the Kiowas
have relatives in the night sky, watching over us. And so, my
grandmother told me, we Kiowas are never alone in the night.

40   Although my grandmother was a Christian in her later years, she
never lost her reverence[6] for the sun. As a child she had been to the
Sun Dances and had taken part in those annual rites. She was seven
when the last Kiowa Sun Dance was held in 1887. The old men had
to travel all the way to Texas to beg for a buffalo head to hang on the
45 sacred tree, because all the buffalo on the Plains were gone. Three
years later, they had to settle for an old buffalo hide. Before that
ceremony could begin, soldiers rode out from Fort Sill with orders
to disperse[7] the tribe. Without bitterness, and for as long as she
lived, my grandmother carried the memory of the death of her
50 people's sun god.

    Now my grandmother lives only in my memory. I remember her
standing at the wood stove on a winter morning; sitting at the
window bent over her beadwork; and later, when her eyesight failed,
just looking at her hands. I remember her most often at prayer.

55   The last time I saw her pray, she stood at her bedside in the
lamplight. I do not speak Kiowa, and I never understood her prayers,
but there was something inherently[8] sad in the sound of the words.

    Again and again she began on a high note that went lower and
lower until she was out of breath. In the dancing light among the
60 shadows of her room, she seemed beyond the reach of time. I knew
then that I should not see her again.

---

6. **reverence** (REHV uhr uhns): deep respect, mixed with fear and love.
7. **disperse** (dihs PURS): drive off in different directions; scatter.
8. **inherently** (in HIHR ehnt lee): basically; innately; as inborn.

Once there was a lot of sound in my grandmother's house, a lot of coming and going, feasting and talk. Visitors came in the summer, old people who walked straight and proud. The men wore great black hats and big, bright shirts. Some painted their faces and wound their braids with strips of colored cloth. The women wore fringed and flowered shawls, bright beadwork, and German silver. There were prayer meetings and great nighttime feasts. We children played outside, and the singing of the old people rose and carried into the night. There were a lot of good things to eat and a lot of laughter. Later, when it was quiet, I lay down with my grandmother, and I could hear the frogs down by the river.

Now there is only silence in the rooms of her house. It was late at night when I returned, and there was a moon, almost full, in the sky. I sat a long time on the stone steps by the kitchen door. Once I looked at the moon and saw a strange thing. A cricket had perched upon the handrail, only a few inches from me. My line of sight made it seem that the cricket filled the moon, looking like a fossil[9] there. It had gone to the moon, I thought, to live and die. There, of all places, its smallness was made large and eternal.[10] A warm wind rose up and moved in ripples like the longing deep within me.

The next morning, I awoke at dawn and went out on the dirt road to Rainy Mountain. It was already hot, and the grasshoppers began to fill the air. Birds sang in the shadows. And there was my grandmother's grave, surrounded by dark stones with ancestral names on them. Looking back once, I saw the mountain and came away.

---

9. **fossil** (FOS uhl): hardened remains of an animal or plant from a long time ago.
10. **eternal** (ih TUR nuhl): timeless; always and forever the same.

Setting

Where does a story take place? **When** does it happen? These are the two basic questions you ask yourself when you are thinking about setting— the place and time of a story. The setting can also affect other parts of a story, such as the atmosphere, or mood. So you can also ask yourself, "What is the **mood** created by this setting? How does the writer's description of setting make me feel?"

The chart below lists some of the settings described in *The Way to Rainy Mountain.* Complete the chart by describing the mood that is created by each setting. Use details from the memoir to explain your answer. Number 2 has been done for you.

#1	#2
Place: Rainy Mountain, Oklahoma **Time:** Both when the writer visits and at the time of his ancestors **Mood:**	**Place:** Devils Tower, Wyoming **Time:** Both when the writer visits and at the time of his ancestors **Mood:** quiet, spiritual, larger than us, peaceful, kind of scary. These words come to my mind because the writer tells the Kiowa legend of Devils Tower, where the sisters are playing and are chased by a bear. They run away from the bear up to the sky and become the stars of the Big Dipper. Also the writer says the place creates an "awesome quiet" in people.
#3	#4
Place: Grandmother's House **Time:** When the writer is a child **Mood:**	**Place:** Grandmother's House **Time:** When the writer visits as a grown-up **Mood:**

AUTHOR AND TITLE INDEX